BRITISH RAILWAYS

PAST and PRESENT

No 43

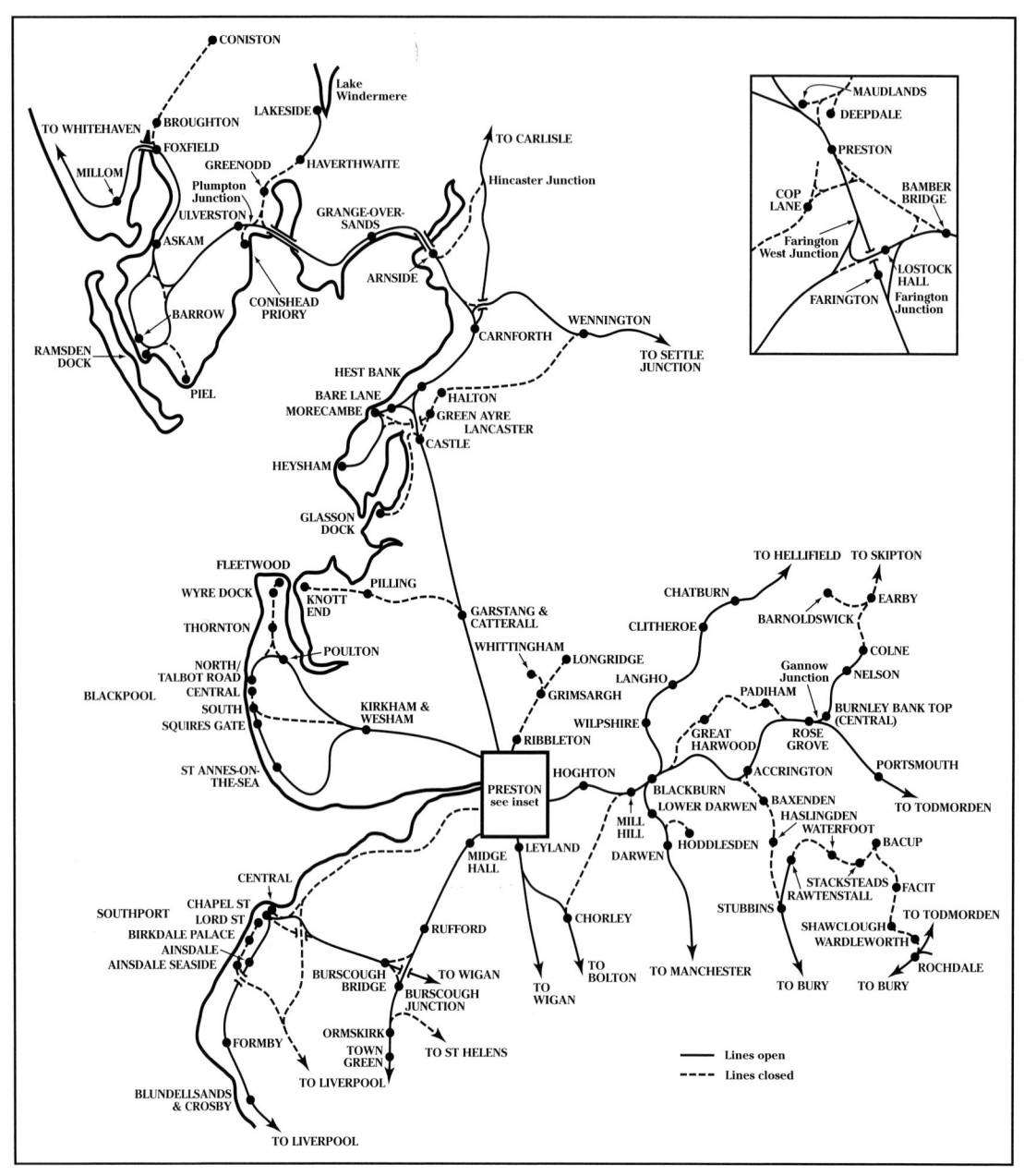

Map of the area covered by this book.

BRITISH RAILWAYS
PAST and PRESENT

No 43
West, East and North Lancashire

Paul Shannon & John Hillmer

Past & Present Publishing Ltd

© Paul Shannon & John Hillmer 2004

All rights reserved. No part of this publication may be reproduced, stored in a retrieval system or transmitted, in any form or by any means, electronic, mechanical, photocopying, recording or otherwise, without prior permission in writing from Past & Present Publishing Ltd.

First published in 2004
Reprinted in 2010

British Library Cataloguing in Publication Data

A catalogue record for this book is available from the British Library.

ISBN 978 1 85895 237 6
Past & Present Publishing Ltd
The Trundle
Ringstead Road
Great Addington
Kettering
Northants NN14 4BW

Tel/Fax: 01536 330588
email: sales@nostalgiacollection.com
Website: www.nostalgiacollection.com

Printed and bound in Czech Republic

AINSDALE BEACH was opened by the CLC in 1901 as 'Seaside' and renamed in 1912. It never had goods facilities. In this undated photo, the line runs between the hotel and station building behind the signal box, which opened on 16 December 1900. A short train from Southport is in the station and waits for the signal; the loco looks like a 'D5' 4-4-0.

The CLC line to Southport closed in 1952. On 24 June 2003, looking across the roundabout, the Sands Hotel appears much the same and the railway building remains on the right, but the former trackbed is now a road leading to Southport.
John Ryan collection/JCH

CONTENTS

Introduction	7
Southport and West Lancashire	8
Preston	24
East Lancashire	39
The Fylde	74
Around Lancaster	90
Furness	110
Index of locations	128

BIBLIOGRAPHY

150 Years of the Lancashire & Yorkshire Railway *by Noel Coates* (Hawkshill Publishing)
ABC British Railways Locomotives, combined volumes: various years (Ian Allan)
ABC Railway Freight Operations *by Paul Shannon* (Ian Allan)
BR Steam Motive Power Depots: LMR *by Paul Bolger* (Ian Allan)
BR Track Diagrams: No 4 London Midland Region (Quail Map Co)
The Cheshire Lines Committee *by Paul Bolger* (Heyday Publishing)
Complete British Railways Maps and Gazetteer 1830-1981 *by C. J. Wignall* (OPC)
Directory of British Engine Sheds 2 *by Roger Griffiths and Paul Smith* (OPC)
The Directory of Railway Stations *by R. V. J. Butt* (Patrick Stephens)
Freight Only Yearbook Nos 1 and 2 *by Michael Rhodes and Paul Shannon* (Silver Link Publishing)
The Furness Railway Vol 1 *by K. J. Norman* (Silver Link Publishing)
The Lancashire & Yorkshire Railway *by Alan Earnshaw* (Ian Allan)

Old Ordnance Survey Maps: various (Alan Godfrey Maps)
Pennine Branch Lines *by Alan Earnshaw* (Ian Allan)
A Pictorial Survey of Railway Signalling *by D. Allen and C. J. Woolstenholmes* (OPC)
Rail Atlas of Great Britain and Ireland *by S. K. Baker*: various editions (OPC)
Railways of Blackpool & the Fylde *by Barry McLoughlin* (Silver Link Publishing)
A Regional History of the Railways of Great Britain: Volume 10 The North West *by Geoffrey O. Holt* (David & Charles)
Regional Railway Centres: North West *by Rex Christiansen* (Ian Allan)
Steam Motive Power Depots: Volume 3 *by Paul Smith* (Platform Five Publishing)

Back issues of:
Branch Line News
Modern Railways
Rail
Railway Magazine
The Railway Observer
Railway World

LANCASTER CASTLE: On 20 April 1968, the fateful year when steam ended, 'Black Five' 4-6-0 No 45435 speeds through with the 1335 SO Darwen-Heysham oil tanks. 'Sister' engine No 44942 stands on the right.

Although the Heysham branch today sees little freight use, the West Coast Main Line is still a busy freight artery. On 29 August 2003 Class 56 No 56118 heads north with an infrastructure train. Apart from the electrification masts and wires very little appears to have changed in the 35 years between the two photographs.
Tom Heavyside/JCH

INTRODUCTION

The Lancashire railway system falls broadly into three categories: the strategic West Coast Main Line (WCML), secondary inter-urban routes and rural branches. Each category has evolved in a different way: the WCML has been modernised and upgraded, many inter-urban routes have been either rationalised or closed, and the rural branches – few as they were in the county – have been abandoned. These changes are represented graphically in the pairs of pictures that make up this book; today's scenes range from 21st-century 'Voyagers' to long-abandoned and sometimes redeveloped trackbeds.

The WCML is arguably the only railway route in the region where most of the traffic – both passenger and freight – is merely passing through. That fact is reflected in the state of the line today: the tracks have been upgraded and electrified, but the smaller intermediate stations have closed. The two principal stations that remain – Preston and Lancaster – have been successfully adapted to today's traffic needs, while retaining much of their 19th-century character. As for freight, the West Coast Main Line carries a higher tonnage than the rest of the railway network of North Lancashire put together, even though hardly any of that tonnage originates or terminates in the county.

The principal inter-urban routes include those serving the former coal and cotton towns of East Lancashire as well as those serving seaside resorts such as Southport, Blackpool and Morecambe. In East Lancashire the railway network followed the same fortunes as the industries it served: hasty expansion in the mid-19th century was followed by a period of stability, followed in turn by rapid decline in the 1950s and '60s. The main artery from Preston to Colne survives, but heavily rationalised and with most stations reduced to unstaffed halts. The remaining lines to Southport and Blackpool have been simplified too: gone are the days when most holidaymakers and daytrippers made their journey by train. The surviving Furness Railway route to Barrow is unusual among Lancashire's secondary lines in still carrying freight as well as passengers.

Truly rural branch lines in Lancashire were already an endangered species before most of the 'past' photographs in this book were taken. The branches to Longridge and Knott End were early victims of road competition, as was the meandering Cheshire Lines Committee approach to Southport. The 1950s and '60s put paid to remaining rural and semi-rural outposts such as Barnoldswick, Coniston and Lakeside, even though the last-mentioned location survives as a tourist attraction.

The business of identifying and revisiting former railway locations after a gap of half a century or more is always fascinating, even if scenes of neglect and abandonment are all too common. We are grateful to the many photographers and holders of photographic collections who allowed us to reproduce their material; we also wish to record special thanks to Bryan Wilson, Richard Casserley, Michael Ellis, Allan Lewis, Barry McLoughlin and the *Blackpool Gazette*.

John Hillmer, Wilmslow
Paul Shannon, Chester

Southport and West Lancashire

Southport was reached first by the Liverpool, Crosby & Southport Railway, which opened Eastbank Street station in 1848 and moved to Chapel Street in 1851. The company amalgamated with the Lancashire & Yorkshire Railway in 1855. Chapel Street was also used by the Manchester & Southport Railway, which arrived from Wigan in 1855. The East Lancashire Railway, although sharing the line from Burscough Bridge, had its own terminus in London Street, which closed in 1857 (with later usage by excursions). Chapel Street was then rebuilt and extended to absorb London Street. In 1882 Southport Central station was opened as the terminus of the West Lancashire Railway line from Preston. The WLR was absorbed by the L&YR in 1897 and Central station closed in 1901.

In 1884 another terminal station was opened in Lord Street, which had become one of the most prestigious shopping streets in North West England. This was used by the Cheshire Lines Committee, under the auspices of the Southport & Cheshire Lines Extension. This was the only company in the area that did not ultimately find itself part of the Lancashire & Yorkshire.

The ever-increasing popularity of the town as a seaside resort was proven by the fact that for a short period it was served by three separate railways, each having its own terminus – indeed, until the 1890s the town attracted more visitors than its rival Lancashire resort of Blackpool. The line from Liverpool via Crosby was electrified in 1904, Chapel Street station was enlarged in 1901, and in 1911 an additional approach was added from Wigan via the Blowick curve.

Fast trains to Manchester included the so-called 'Club Train' for wealthy business commuters, although no special carriages were used. By 1939 the Flower Show had become the largest in the world, bringing more excursion traffic. But once the usage of private cars started to increase after the Second World War, there was a decline in passenger traffic on the railways, and Lord Street closed in 1952. Through coaches between Southport and London Euston, via Liverpool, ceased in 1966..

Today the electrified line from Liverpool brings large numbers of visitors to the town and enables many Southport residents to commute into Liverpool. There is currently a frequent service of four trains an hour during the day and more at peak times. All services from Southport go to Liverpool Central and many continue to Hunts Cross. On the Wigan line, there are two trains an hour to Manchester or beyond.

Opposite page BLUNDELLSANDS & CROSBY: Opened as 'Crosby' in 1848 by the Liverpool, Crosby & Southport Railway, the station became 'Crosby & Blundellsands' in 1852, before acquiring its current name in 1878. Laid out in the 19th century as a high-class residential area, the town has retained much of its character. Electrification took place in 1904, an example of excellent forward thinking by the L&YR. In this close-up view of the station a number of passengers are awaiting the arrival of the approaching unit. These trains operated in fixed formations, the notice on the right-hand side stating 'Third class smoking here'. Further down the platform a member of the staff is up a ladder attending to one of the platform lamps.

In today's photograph, taken on 24 June 2003, the canopies have been swept away but the station buildings on the up side remain intact. Class 508 No 508125 is arriving from Southport en route to Liverpool and Hunts Cross.
Mike Hitches collection/JCH

FORMBY station was originally known as 'Formby & Altcar' and renamed Formby in 1866. It served a desirable residential community for Liverpool businessmen and their families. In the post-1904 picture, at least four members of staff stand on the up platform as a two-coach train approaches the substantial station buildings. The view was taken from the elevated booking office at the north end. The station was rebuilt in 1910 by the L&YR. Careful inspection reveals that the two platforms were going to be changed into 'islands', but in practice it never happened.

The L&YR buildings are still in place to greet the arrival of Class 507 No 507031 on a Liverpool-bound working on 10 June 2003. *Mike Hitches collection/JCH*

The rather nice name inset on the outside of the station. *JCH*

AINSDALE serves a pleasant residential area a few miles south of Southport. Looking north, in this photograph dated around 1917, a permanent way gang is working on the down side, as a Liverpool-bound unit approaches on the other track.

Unusually, as can be seen in the 'present' picture taken on 24 June 2003, trees have been cut back, revealing more buildings, including one with a small tower, the top of which can be seen above a tree in the 'past' photograph. The lower-quadrant semaphore has long been replaced by colour light signalling. Class 507 No 507016 prepares to stop with a Hunts Cross service. *John Ryan collection/JCH*

CHAPEL STREET (1) replaced Eastbank Street, the first terminus of the Liverpool, Crosby & Southport Railway, in 1851. It was shared with the East Lancashire Railway when rebuilt and enlarged in 1901. The last L&YR 2-4-2T in service, No 50850, is hauling out a rake of empty stock on 24 August 1961. This Aspinall-designed engine was introduced in 1910, so it had celebrated its half-century.

Since the end of steam in 1968, most services on the non-electric side of the station have been operated by DMUs, although for a period there were loco-hauled morning and evening trains between Southport and Manchester. The overall train sheds remain, as seen in the present picture taken on 10 June 2003, although they are no longer glazed. *Ian Holt/JCH*

CHAPEL STREET (2): The imposing frontage of the station is seen around 1900, advertising direct services to Liverpool, Manchester, Leeds, Bradford, Halifax and 'all parts of Yorkshire'.
  When the entrance to the station was incorporated into a shopping mall, the original exterior was demolished and replaced by an unattractive concrete one, as seen on 10 June 2003. *J. K. Williams collection/JCH*

BIRKDALE PALACE station was located just over a mile from Lord Street on the CLC route, and opened at the same time as the line in 1884. In this view, taken around 1910 looking towards Southport, above the station on the skyline can just be seen the tower of Lord Street station. A rake of six-wheeled coaches is stabled in the station.

The course of the railway has completely disappeared under new roads, but the houses to the right of the station remain as they were, as photographed on 24 June 2003. *J. K. Williams collection/JCH*

LORD STREET: The Southport & Cheshire Lines Extension brought the CLC into the town in 1884. Fronting on to the fashionable shopping street, the station had five platform faces and close by was a goods depot and small two-road engine shed. Taken on 29 July 1951, this photograph shows the platform extensions and the upper-quadrant semaphores, while in the station an ex-Midland Railway 4-4-0 lets off steam.

The station closed in 1952, and from 1954 until 1987 was used as a bus station by Ribble, followed by an unsuccessful shopping centre. There is now a supermarket where the main station was situated, but the tower remains, as seen in the photograph dated 10 June 2003. *John Ward collection/JCH*

BURSCOUGH BRIDGE lies on the Wigan-Southport line and was once a three-way junction with north- and south-facing connections to the Preston-Ormskirk line. On 26 August 1964 'Black Five' 4-6-0 No 45409 approaches the station with the 5.10pm Manchester Victoria-Southport 'Club Train'. The Preston curve is visible on the left and the Ormskirk curve on the right.

In the intermediate photo, taken on 8 June 1984, a two-car Class 108 DMU comprising M51917 and M54502 forms the 1610 service from Manchester Victoria to Southport. The junction to the left has gone, although the line of trees and bushes show where it ran, while the single-track spur to the right remains in position, albeit disused since 1982.

In today's photograph, taken on 3 July 2003, the right-hand junction has also been removed. Class 142 No 142001 passes the box with the 1226 Rochdale to Southport service. The signal box retains its original name, although no junction remains. *John Ward collection/PDS/JCH*

CHAPEL STREET (3): Caprotti Class 5 4-6-0 No 44686 leaves the station with a three-coach train on 28 June 1964. Nos 44686 and 44687 were the last two Class 5s to be built, and the only members of the class to have high running-boards and a double chimney. Over to the right, above the tracks, is a sign stating 'London Street – excursion platforms'.

Comparison with the photo taken on 10 June 2003, with First North Western-operated 'Sprinter' No 150222 arriving with the 1026 service from Rochdale, shows that the area to the right has been turned into a car-park. *John Ward collection/JCH*

SOUTHPORT L&YR SHED AND YARD: Close to the station on the up side was the L&YR loco shed. A substantial six-road building, it remained operational until 1966, and was then preserved for a number of years as the headquarters of 'Steamtown'. In the line-up of engines dated 17 May 1964 are several Class 5 4-6-0s, two 2-6-0 'Crabs' and a 2-6-4T.

Between the station and the loco shed were the extensive goods sidings. The shed building can be seen on the left-hand side of the picture and retail coal sidings in the foreground.

Subsequently the whole area was redeveloped and is now a large shopping complex, as seen in the 'present' photo of 10 June 2003. *John Ward collection/J. K. Williams collection/JCH*

CENTRAL station was opened in 1882 as the Southport terminus of the West Lancashire Railway. This company was absorbed into the L&YR in 1897 and Central station closed to passengers four years later. It had rather an imposing frontage, as seen in this undated photograph. The adjacent goods yard became part of Kensington Road goods depot, which survived until 1973.

After demolition and construction of the shopping centre, the original name of Central is commemorated at the top of the list of shops on the site, seen in the photo dated 10 June 2003. *J. K. Williams collection/JCH*

RUFFORD: The Preston-Ormskirk line was singled in 1970 and Rufford became the only passing place. On 31 August 1985 a two-car unit formed of M52061 and M51920 passes the delightful signal box as it comes off the single line from Midge Hall and runs into the platform with a Preston-Ormskirk service.

On 22 July 2003 Class 153 No 153324 approaches the station with the 1302 service from Preston to Ormskirk. The old crossing gates have been replaced by barriers, the signal box was ousted in 1985 by a Portakabin on the Preston platform, and the semaphore signals have given way to colour lights. The signalling method is 'electric token block' from Midge Hall to Rufford, and one-train working with train staff from Rufford to Ormskirk. The signalman will stand on the platform to hand the driver the staff for the Ormskirk section once the train has stopped. *PDS/JCH*

BURSCOUGH JUNCTION station was opened in 1849 by the Liverpool, Ormskirk & Preston Railway, soon to be amalgamated with the East Lancashire Railway and later absorbed by the L&YR. On 27 August 1964 Class 5 4-6-0 No 44733, allocated to Blackpool (10B at that time), draws into the station with the 3.15pm Windermere-Liverpool train.

The line was singled in 1970 and the station is a shadow of its former self, with just a single platform and 'bus-stop'-type waiting shelter. The buildings, canopies and footbridge have all been swept away. Single-car Class 153 No 153361, allocated to Newton Heath depot (NH), arrives on 3 July 2003 from the Preston direction en route to Ormskirk. There is a two-hourly service from Mondays to Saturdays, but no Sunday service. *John Ward collection/JCH*

ORMSKIRK: Looking north from the road overbridge, we see the expanse of the station in L&YR days, with a small goods yard to the left, a bay on the other side and substantial platforms. In the bay is an L&YR 0-4-0 Railmotor (10600-10617 series) with a Maghull service. In 1910 the 'Maghull Motor' ran 16 times a day Monday-Saturday and eight times on Sundays. Out of sight at the far end on the east side, the line from St Helens ran in from the north.

All we have now is a single platform with a Liverpool-bound electric unit awaiting departure from the south end and a Preston service formed of Class 153 No 153361 ready to head north. The track is severed by buffer stops between the two trains, making the station a double terminus. *J. K. Williams collection/JCH*

TOWN GREEN station was renamed Town Green & Aughton in 1889 but reverted to its original title in 1975. In this postcard date-stamped 1910 and looking towards Ormskirk, there are two rather nattily dressed passengers wearing straw boaters! The station facilities include a 'Ladies Room Third Class' and a 'Gentlemen's Room First Class'! It would be 1913 before the line was electrified.

Although nearly 100 years have passed since the original photograph was taken, there has been remarkably little change. The semaphore signals have been replaced by colour lights and a new footbridge has been put in place, but the station building on the up side is much the same, although the facilities for passengers are greatly reduced. Merseyrail electric No 507006 approaches with an Ormskirk-Liverpool service on 3 July 2003. *John Ryan collection/JCH*

Preston

Preston gained its first railway in 1838, when the North Union Railway opened its line from Warrington. The strategic importance of this opening was huge, as it gave Preston direct links with Liverpool, Manchester, Birmingham and London. It was not long before the tracks continued northwards: the Lancaster & Preston Junction Railway and the Preston & Wyre Railway both opened in 1840. That same year also saw the opening of the Preston & Longridge Railway – a smaller, self-contained operation intended mainly to carry building stone from Longridge Fell.

The completion of the Bolton & Preston Railway in 1843 gave Preston a shorter railway route to Manchester, while the East Lancashire Railway opened its lines to Blackburn in 1846 and to Liverpool in 1849. The final addition to Preston's main-line railway network was the arrival of the West Lancashire Railway from Southport in 1882. The last-mentioned line originally had its own terminus at Preston, although from 1900 passenger trains from Southport used the North Union station.

By the end of the 19th century, amalgamations had brought Preston's railway network under the control of just two companies, the LNWR and the L&YR. They too were amalgamated in 1921, just ahead of the Grouping. However the L&YR (ex-East Lancashire Railway) platforms at Preston remained a distinct part of the station until their closure in 1972.

The first significant line closure in the Preston area was the withdrawal of the Longridge branch passenger service in 1930. The Beeching era brought further cutbacks: the Southport line closed in 1964 and the complex network of junctions and connections in the Farington area was rationalised by the early 1970s. Freight facilities were gradually withdrawn as the operation of pick-up goods trains became uneconomic. The only rail freight terminal around Preston in 2003 is the TotalFinaElf bitumen depot in Preston Docks, about to be revived after eight years of disuse.

Resignalling and electrification changed the face of Preston's railways in the early 1970s. Numerous small signal boxes were abolished and Preston lost its impressive semaphore signal gantries. Within five years, from 1968 to 1973, the area changed from being one of the last outposts of BR standard gauge steam to enjoying the very latest in main-line electric traction. That traction was, however, to last 30 years in front-line service; only now in 2003 are 'Pendolino' units taking over West Coast expresses.

PENWORTHAM COP LANE: BR Standard Class 2 2-6-0 No 78041 calls at Penwortham Cop Lane with the 2.34pm Preston-Southport train on 6 September 1964. The headboard confirms that this was the last day of operation on the Preston-Southport line. Cop Lane was a simple halt without goods facilities, opened by the L&YR in 1911.

The former trackbed through Penwortham is now occupied by the A582, one of a number of new roads built to cater for late-20th-century housing and commercial development on the south side of Preston. The 'present' photograph is dated 26 May 2003. *J. K. Williams collection/PDS*

25

LEYLAND: Ex-LMS 'Royal Scot' 4-6-0 No 46115 *Scots Guardsman* passes Leyland with an afternoon train from Blackpool on 13 July 1963. No 46115 was the last 'Royal Scot' to remain in BR stock, running until December 1965, and was one of only two 'Royal Scots' to survive into preservation, based first at Dinting Railway Centre and later at Tyseley. It currently resides at the Railway Age, Crewe.

Overhead wires and masts clutter today's view of the railway at Leyland, while the small parcel of land on the up side has been filled with housing. Direct Rail Services locos Nos 37611 and 37609 head south with 4Z30, the 1138 Carlisle-Daventry intermodal service, on 26 May 2003. This was a Bank Holiday Monday and the appearance of a freight train was unexpected. *Ian Holt/PDS*

FARINGTON (1): Steam meets diesel on the West Coast Main Line: an unidentified 'Black Five' heads north with a down 'special' at Farington Junction in the early 1960s, while an English Electric Type 4 (later Class 40) heads south with an up express.

The track layout at Farington was modified in the 1970s to allow trains to cross over between the slow lines, nearest the photographer, and the up-side spur to Lostock Hall. First North Western unit No 158752 forms the 1435 Manchester Airport-Blackpool North service on 26 May 2003. The railway is more securely fenced than in the earlier picture. *Keith Sanders/PDS*

FARINGTON (2): This early 1960s view shows a Metropolitan-Cammell diesel multiple-unit passing Farington Junction on the up fast line, while a Stanier 8F awaits the right of way with an engineers' train on the down slow. The sidings on both sides contain a fine assortment of wooden- and steel-bodied coal wagons.

The 1538 Lancaster-London Euston passes the remodelled Farington Junction on 26 May 2003. The spur to Lostock Hall, to the right, is still open but has no regular traffic at the time of writing apart from a twice-weekly 'Enterprise' freight between Warrington and Blackburn. The two overgrown sidings on the extreme right were formerly used for exchanging electric and diesel locomotives, especially on passenger trains diverted via the Settle to Carlisle line. *Keith Sanders/PDS*

LOSTOCK HALL (1): Two ex-LMS 8F 2-8-0 locomotives, Nos 48345 and 48550, pass Lostock Hall Junction with a train of track panels from Fazakerley to the north via the Settle to Carlisle line on 9 July 1967. By this time about 200 8Fs remained in service, concentrated mainly in the North West. The photograph shows many steam-age railway features that would soon be swept away by modernisation.

First North Western unit No 150143 has just departed from the re-sited Lostock Hall station with the 0900 Blackpool South-Colne train; the little-used Farington Curve diverges to the left; the rails on both lines having a thick coating of rust on 26 May 2003. *Tom Heavyside/PDS*

LOSTOCK HALL (2): Fairburn 2-6-4T No 42158 calls at Lostock Hall station with the 11.5am Liverpool-Blackpool on 22 August 1960. The adjacent shed with its massive coaling tower was to become one of the last strongholds of BR steam, closing at the same time as Rose Grove on 5 August 1968.

The original Lostock Hall station closed in 1969, while parts of the former steam shed remained in use by BR's Carriage & Wagon Department until 1988. The second photograph shows No 47409 hauling the diverted 0725 Nottingham-Glasgow service on 29 March 1986. By this time BR had built a new Lostock Hall station, located behind the photographer on the other side of the road bridge.

Today the former shed site appears ripe for redevelopment. Unit No 158768 hurries past with the 0847 Blackpool North to York service on 26 May 2003. *R. S. Greenwood/PDS (2)*

PRESTON EAST LANCS: The East Lancashire Railway opened its own platforms on the east side at Preston in 1850, abutting the existing North Union station but with independent access from Lostock Hall and Bamber Bridge. The two parts of the station remained in separate ownership until the L&YR and LNWR were amalgamated in 1921, but the side platforms were still referred to as 'Preston East Lancs' in the BR era. Ex-War Department Class 8F 2-8-0 No 90160 awaits the road with a southbound engineers' train on 30 August 1964.

The East Lancs platforms and the connecting line from Bamber Bridge were closed in 1972, with trains to and from Blackburn being diverted via Lostock Hall and Farington West Junction. The closure released a large area of land for retail development and car parking, as pictured on 26 May 2003. *Noel A. Machell/PDS*

PRESTON (1): The original Preston station of 1838 soon became inadequate for the expanding railway network of central Lancashire and in 1880 a greatly enlarged station was completed on the same site. Most of the passenger facilities were concentrated on a lengthy island platform, reached by a ramp from nearby Fishergate. 'Black Five' No 45134 calls at the down side of the island platform with a short parcels train on 26 February 1968.

Forty-five years later the changes are subtle rather than dramatic. Even the overhead electrification equipment is inconspicuous. 'Voyager' unit No 220008 draws to a halt ready to form the 0830 departure to Plymouth on 26 May 2003. *Roger Siviter/PDS*

PRESTON (2): Until the early 1970s Preston station boasted a fine selection of semaphore signal gantries. This view, looking south, shows 'Black Five' No 44761 heading an up goods train on 26 February 1968, while a diesel shunter manoeuvres a short rake of parcels vans.

The track layout at Preston was greatly simplified with resignalling and electrification in the early 1970s. First North Western 'Sprinter' No 150143 arrives with the 0716 Colne-Blackpool South service on 26 May 2003. The track on the far right, outside the signal gantry, gives access to Preston Docks and was awaiting re-opening as this book went to press. *Roger Siviter/PDS*

DEEPDALE: The original Longridge branch terminus at Preston Deepdale closed to passengers after the connecting line to Maudlands (Preston & Wyre Railway) was opened in 1856. Deepdale then enjoyed a long life as a goods station, finally becoming a coal concentration depot. Signs of dilapidation are evident as Nos 20094 and 20080 shunt HEA coal hoppers at Deepdale on 2 August 1985, having worked 6P81, the 1115 'special' from Warrington Walton Old Junction.

Deepdale coal depot outlived most others of its type and was still receiving occasional rail-borne traffic in the early 1990s, despite the poor state of the track and with ever worsening problems with vandalism on the 1½-mile branch from Preston station. Bizarrely, only after its closure was the branch enclosed by high-security fencing, as pictured on 26 May 2003. Locomotive No 20094 passed into preservation and is based at Barrow Hill at the time of writing. *Both PDS*

GRIMSARGH: A small private railway opened in 1889 from Grimsargh to Whittingham Mental Hospital, designed to bring the hospital's supplies of coal and other goods but also carrying a free passenger service for hospital staff and visitors. At Grimsargh the hospital branch had its own platform, located on the opposite side of the level crossing from the Longridge branch station. On 19 June 1948 0-4-2T No 2, built by Andrew Barclay of Kilmarnock in 1904, prepares to take a party of enthusiasts along the 2-mile hospital branch. The Longridge branch is sandwiched between the wooden fences on the left.

The Whittingham branch remained in operation until Lancashire County Council closed it in 1957, some 27 years after connecting services on the Longridge branch had ceased. Today, as seen on 26 May 2003, the study of a large-scale map is necessary to identify the location. *A. Appleton, courtesy John Ward/PDS*

WHITTINGHAM: The generously roofed passenger platform at Whittingham Mental Hospital is pictured on 21 April 1951, looking towards Grimsargh. The track continued behind the photographer to provide access to the engine shed and sidings in the hospital grounds.

A return visit on 26 March 2003, some 46 years after the closure of the railway, found the trackbed heavily overgrown but traceable, the low brick wall and building on the right providing definite links with the 'past' picture. Some former railway buildings, not visible in this photograph, were taken over by the health authority as workshops and stores, but much of the site awaits redevelopment as a housing estate. *H. C. Casserley/ PDS*

The third photograph shows the traction used on the line after 1947: former Southern Railway 0-4-2T No 2357, built in 1886 as London, Brighton & South Coast Railway No 357 *Riddlesdown*. *H. C. Casserley*

LONGRIDGE: The 6-mile Longridge branch was opened as early as 1840 to carry high-quality building stone from Longridge Fell to Preston. Horse-drawn trains gave way to steam in 1848 and a connection with the Preston & Wyre Railway was opened soon afterwards, but proposals to create an extension from Longridge to Clitheroe were never realised and the branch led a quiet existence until its passenger service ended in 1930. The line then became a desirable goal for enthusiasts' specials. and here ex-LNWR Class G2 0-8-0 No 49451 runs round a Railway Correspondence & Travel Society railtour in the station area on 22 September 1962. The tender wheels are remarkably close to the point blades, which have not yet been switched for the direction of travel awaiting the opening of the level crossing gates.

The Longridge branch closed beyond the Courtaulds works at Ribbleton (Red Scar) in 1967. The section from Deepdale to Red Scar closed in 1980, leaving just the coal concentration depot at Deepdale to eke out a meagre existence until the early 1990s. At Longridge, the Towneley Arms Hotel still overlooks the site of the level crossing, as pictured on **26 May 2003**. *Noel A. Machell/PDS*

East Lancashire

Coal and cotton brought prosperity to a huge swathe of East Lancashire by the end of the 19th century. Villages grew rapidly into towns, and the lower slopes of the Pennines were covered with seemingly endless rows of houses and mills. This was promising territory for the early railway builders: between 1846 and 1852 a network of lines was completed serving Blackburn (from both Bolton and Preston), Bacup, Accrington (from Blackburn and Bury), Burnley and Colne. The network also catered for trans-Pennine traffic with links from Burnley to Todmorden and from Colne to Skipton. Later additions included the Padiham loop and the extension of the line from Clitheroe to Hellifield. Unlike many parts of the country, there was little opportunity for inter-company rivalry: almost all routes were worked by the East Lancashire Railway, the main exception being the Colne-Skipton line, which belonged to the Midland Railway.

Despite the large centres of population and industry, the railways of East Lancashire were geared more to local than to long-distance traffic. Most Anglo-Scottish passenger traffic was channelled via Preston, with the theoretical alternative route via Bolton, Blackburn and Hellifield failing to catch on. The natural topography of Bacup and the Rossendale Valley ensured that their railways were never more than branch lines.

Industrial decline and the growth of road transport began to eat into the railway's revenues in the 1950s. The later additions to the East Lancashire network were among the first closures: the Rochdale-Bacup branch lost its passenger service in 1947, followed by the Padiham loop in 1957 and the Hellifield line in 1962. The Burnley-Todmorden link lost its local passenger service but remained in use by holiday trains.

Post-Beeching closures included the Barnoldswick branch in 1965, Rawtenstall-Bacup and Stubbins-Accrington in 1966 and Colne-Skipton in 1970. The main corridor from Preston to Burnley and Todmorden was resignalled in the early 1970s, but Victorian signalling methods remained in use on the Colne branch – until it was singled in 1986 – and on the Clitheroe line.

Today the railways of East Lancashire are diesel unit territory. The only active freight terminals are Clitheroe cement works and the Gilbraith distribution depot at Blackburn – and the latter was receiving very little traffic when this book went to press. But the passenger network is larger than it was in the 1970s, thanks to the re-introduction of regular all-year-round services on the Burnley-Todmorden line in 1984 and to Clitheroe in 1994.

HODDLESDEN JUNCTION marked the divergence of the short goods-only Hoddlesden branch from the Blackburn-Bolton line, operational from 1876 until 1950. With the overgrown tracks of Hollins goods depot visible beyond the ex-L&YR box, 'Black Five' 4-6-0s Nos 44874 and 45017 pass the former junction with an enthusiasts' special on 4 August 1968.

Hoddlesden Junction box was replaced in 1973 by a ground frame, which continued to control access to Hoddlesden goods loop and the adjacent oil terminal. The ground frame was finally removed in 1993, some time after the oil traffic had ceased. Unit No 150135 forms the 1439 Clitheroe-Manchester Victoria service on 29 March 2003. *Hugh Ballantyne/PDS*

LOWER DARWEN station is pictured looking towards Bolton on 11 April 1957, less than two years before its closure to passengers. It served a mainly rural area between the industrial towns of Blackburn and Darwen and can never have attracted large volumes of traffic. The L&YR had a locomotive shed named Lower Darwen, but this was located about half a mile further north.

On 29 March 2003 just a single track remains, with a colour light signal controlled from Preston power box. New housing occupies the site of the goods yard. *R. M. Casserley/PDS*

HOGHTON: Much of the line between Preston and Blackburn was rural in nature, but it carried substantial quantities of freight to and from the East Lancashire towns and across the Pennines. Ex-LMS 8F 2-8-0 No 48519 heads east near Hoghton with an unfitted empty coal train from Fleetwood to Rose Grove on 11 April 1968.

At the time of writing only two freight trains a week are booked to pass Hoghton in daylight hours. The Fleetwood branch is closed and Rose Grove is a passenger-only location. 'Pacer' No 142041 heads west with the 1509 Colne-Blackpool South service on 29 March 2003. *Hugh Ballantyne/PDS*

MILL HILL: Located on the western fringe of Blackburn, Mill Hill station was opened by the L&YR in 1887, and was relatively unusual in having an island platform. This turn-of-the-20th-century postcard shows the station looking towards Blackburn. On the left is the goods yard, which was to close as early as 1936.

By 29 March 2003 Mill Hill has been reduced to an unstaffed halt. The mill building just visible on the extreme left of the 'past' picture still stands. *Mike Hitches collection/PDS*

BLACKBURN (1): Blackburn station was rebuilt between 1885 and 1888, and this undated postcard view shows a local train, headed by L&YR 2-4-2T No 10806, entering platform 4.

In the early 1970s all passenger facilities were concentrated on the northernmost island platform, with the shortened platform 4 relegated to emergency use only. Class 25 No 25213 heads west with ballast hoppers on 1 August 1984, while a Birmingham RC&W Co unit headed by car No E53443 waits to depart with the 1612 to Manchester Victoria.

'Pacer' unit No 142009 calls at the much simplified station on 29 March 2003 with the 1209 Colne-Blackpool South service. Platform 4 has been returned to regular use, providing useful flexibility at busy times. *J. K. Williams collection/JCH/ PDS*

BLACKBURN (2): The impressive L&YR station at Blackburn with its twin trainsheds and wealth of architectural detail is shown to good effect in this turn-of-the-20th-century postcard. The clocks were a notable feature; they remained in position for over a century and were rescued for use elsewhere when the station was demolished.

Unit No 158774 calls at the now bi-directional platform 2 with the 1247 Blackpool North-York service on 29 March 2003. At the time of writing an hourly Trans-Pennine Express service operates between Blackpool and York, with alternate trains continuing to Scarborough. *Mike Hitches collection/PDS*

BLACKBURN (3): Three-cylinder Compound 4P 4-4-0 No 41101 stands at platform 1 at Blackburn with the 9.10am from Liverpool on 11 April 1957. This class was introduced in 1924 as a post-Grouping development of the Johnson Midland Compound, and the last two examples were withdrawn in 1961.

The demolition of Blackburn's fine but decaying trainshed in 2000 has altered the feel of the station almost beyond recognition. The new facilities on the main island platform are more practical for today's needs, and the interior of the building is actually more attractive than it appears in this view dated 29 March 2003. *H. C. Casserley/PDS*

BLACKBURN (4): The resignalling and remodelling scheme of the early 1970s left Blackburn with a simplified but asymmetrical track layout. Westbound freight trains generally used the station avoiding line in the foreground, while eastbound services ran through the station. Class 40 No 40136 is in charge of a partly fitted freight train, bound for Carlisle via Settle, on 23 September 1981. BR was to withdraw all through freight traffic from the Settle & Carlisle line in May 1983, and the Class 40 locomotive and vacuum-braked coal hoppers would soon become memories too.

Calling at Blackburn's new station on 29 February 2004 is a Class 150 unit, forming the 1136 Colne-Blackpool South service. The freight-only avoiding line in the foreground now sees little use. *Both PDS*

WILPSHIRE: The Clitheroe line was an important route for goods traffic as it gave access via Hellifield to the Settle & Carlisle line. 'Black Five' 4-6-0 No 44987 heads north through the station with a van train on 1 September 1962.

The station at Wilpshire closed just nine days after the date of the 'past' photograph, when BR withdrew the local passenger service between Blackburn and Hellifield. A visit on 29 March 2003 found the long-disused northbound platform still in position, while a new station has been built on a different site for the resumed local passenger service. *Michael Mensing/PDS*

LANGHO: The L&YR reached Chatburn in 1850, but the all-important extension to Hellifield was not completed until 1880. Thereafter, the Clitheroe line was used for a time by Midland Railway expresses between Manchester and Scotland. This pre-Grouping scene shows a double-headed passenger train calling at Langho, with one Midland Railway clerestory coach followed by a rake of lower-height L&YR coaches.

Langho was the first station on the Blackburn-Hellifield line to close to passenger traffic, in May 1956. BR opened its new station on the same site in 1994, but with staggered platforms because building development had encroached on the site of original up platform. Unit No 150146 calls with the 1631 Clitheroe-Manchester Victoria service on 29 March 2003. *John Ryan collection/PDS*

CLITHEROE: The line from Blackburn to Chatburn required substantial engineering works, notably a 325-yard tunnel at Wilpshire and a 48-arch viaduct at Whalley, yet it served a mainly rural area with limited traffic opportunities. The biggest town along the route was Clitheroe, where the original station is depicted in this fascinating mid-19th-century scene. The wagon of the Tawd Vale Coal Company is worthy of note. The station was rebuilt slightly further north in 1869/70.

Clitheroe was removed from the BR passenger map in 1962, but the retention of the railway for diversions, excursions and freight traffic made it possible to restore local passenger services when circumstances changed. 'Dalesrail' excursions began using the line in 1978; BR introduced a Summer Saturdays service to Clitheroe in 1990; and a regular Blackburn-Clitheroe service calling at three intermediate stations was restored in 1994. *J. K. Williams collection/PDS*

GREAT HARWOOD: The L&YR opened its North Lancashire Loop in 1877, linking Blackburn with Burnley via Great Harwood and Padiham. The neat and tidy station at Great Harwood is pictured in the Edwardian era. At least three of the posters have a travel theme, advertising holidays in the Isle of Man, the ferry service from Hull to Zeebrugge and 'comfortable' travel by the Midland Railway.

The loop line lost its regular passenger service in 1957, but Great Harwood continued to handle goods traffic until 1964, after which the track between Blackburn and Padiham was removed. The former station area at Great Harwood is pictured on 29 March 2003. *John Ryan collection/PDS*

WARDLEWORTH was the first station out of Rochdale on the Rochdale-Bacup branch. This branch was opened as far as Facit in 1870 and extended to Bacup in 1881. Passenger services were withdrawn in 1947, supposedly as a temporary measure due to fuel shortages, but they were never to return. On 15 October 1960 Ivatt 2-6-0 No 46414 is pictured returning from Shawclough & Healey with empty wagons used for conveying bags of asbestos from Salford Docks to Turner's private siding.

Goods traffic on the southern stretch of the branch lasted until 1967. A return visit to Wardleworth on 8 April 2003 found the cutting filled in but Greenbank School still dominating the skyline. *Ian Holt/JCH*

BACUP SHED was located on the Rochdale line, about half a mile from Bacup station. It remained in operation until October 1954, seven years after the Rochdale line lost its passenger service, and latterly was home to about a dozen ex-LMS engines. With the shed building located behind the photographer, Aspinall 2P 2-4-2T No 50887 sets off towards Bacup station for its next duty on 23 April 1954. It was booked to work the 3.54pm to Bury, but was declared a failure before departure and replaced by 0-6-0 No 52443.

The former shed area is now occupied by an industrial estate, as recorded on 15 March 2003. *H. C. Casserley/PDS*

BACUP: Operations on the Rawtenstall-Bacup branch were simplified in 1960, when the section beyond Stacksteads was singled and converted to one-train operation. However, rationalisation did not prevent steam specials from reaching Bacup from time to time. This view from the buffer stops shows Fowler Class 3 2-6-2T No 40063 running round an Roch Valley Railway Society excursion from Manchester Piccadilly on 28 July 1962. Aspinall Class 3F 0-6-0 No 52523 is still attached to the train.

After the branch from Rawtenstall closed in 1966, the site of Bacup station offered a useful piece of flat land for industrial redevelopment in the constricted Rossendale valley. On 15 March 2003 the terraced houses and sturdy stone wall serve to confirm the location. *J. K. Williams collection/PDS*

WATERFOOT: Passenger services between Bury and Bacup went over to DMU operation in February 1956, at a time when diesel traction was a novelty and BR was still (just about!) building steam locomotives. A two-car Metropolitan-Cammell unit approaches Waterfoot station with a Bacup-Bury train shortly after the diesel takeover.

On 15 March 2003 the raised profile of the railway is still discernible in the station area. Most of the stone-built houses beside the main road remain, although a small area has been opened up beside the pedestrian crossing.
J. K. Williams collection/PDS

HASLINGDEN: The East Lancashire Railway opened its link from Stubbins to Accrington in 1848, serving the mill towns of Helmshore and Haslingden. The railway hastened further industrial growth, and the population of Haslingden tripled between 1850 and 1900. This busy scene is believed to date from around 1900.

The heyday of Haslingden was over by the 1950s and the station closed to passengers in 1960. The whole line from Stubbins to Accrington closed in 1966 and the section through Haslingden was taken over by the A56 trunk road. The 'present' scene is dated 15 March 2003. *J. K. Williams collection/PDS*

BAXENDEN: The Stubbins-Accrington line reached a height of 771 feet above sea level near Baxenden, with gradients of between 1 in 38 and 1 in 40 prevailing for 2 of the 3 miles out of Accrington. This postcard of Baxenden Shoe Mill cabin carries a postmark of 13 May 1908, suggesting a turn-of-the-20th-century date for the photograph. The Saxby & Farmer Type 8 cabin was commissioned in 1875/76. What is the man behind the cabin doing?

Shoe Mill cabin was abolished in 1962, four years before the line closed. Much of the trackbed between Accrington and Baxenden now forms a public footpath, as pictured on 29 March 2003. *John Ryan collection/PDS*

ACCRINGTON SHED: Among the locomotives in this 1935 view of Accrington shed are an unidentified ex-L&YR Aspinall 0-6-0 (far left), an unidentified Hughes '5MT' 2-6-0 (second from left), Fowler '4P' 2-6-4T No 2311 (centre) and '2P' 2-4-2T No 10939 (right).

The eight-road dead-end shed was replaced by a six-road building in BR days. That new facility closed to steam in 1961 to become one of the first DMU depots in the country, a role it kept until closure in the 1970s. The cleared and partly redeveloped site is pictured on 29 March 2003. *John Ward* collection/PDS

Opposite page ACCRINGTON (1): Although located at a triangular junction, Accrington station only had two sets of platforms – one set on the east-to-west Colne-Blackburn line and another on the south-to-east curve from Stubbins. Stanier Class 4 2-6-4T No 42655 calls at the main westbound platform with the 5.20pm Colne-Blackpool train on 23 April 1954.

Accrington today is served by hourly stopping trains to and from Colne and by hourly semi-fast services between Blackpool and York via the Copy Pit line. Unit No 158744 forms the 1358 Scarborough-Blackpool North service on 20 February 2003. *H. C. Casserley*/PDS

ACCRINGTON (2): The convergence of the lines from Blackburn and Stubbins at the east end of Accrington station is pictured on 16 April 1973, six months before Preston power box took control of this stretch of the East Lancashire line. Accrington North box was a second-hand L&YR structure installed here in 1939. The line from Stubbins had closed in 1966 but one of the former Stubbins platforms at Accrington remained in use for parcels traffic.

On 20 February 2003 tree growth has obscured much of the townscape visible in the earlier picture, as 'Pacer' No 142027 arrives with the 1609 Colne-Blackpool South service. The 'S'-shaped viaduct, completed in 1867 to replace an earlier structure, is still a prominent feature. *J. K. Williams collection/PDS*

PADIHAM was one of the two principal stopping-places on the 9-mile North Lancashire Loop, which also provided an alternative through route between Blackburn and Burnley. Regular passenger services were withdrawn in 1957, but the Rose Grove to Padiham section remained in use for general coal traffic until 1968 and for access to Padiham power station until the mid-1990s. 'Britannia' 4-6-2 No 70015 *Apollo* passes the disused Padiham station with a Railway Correspondence & Travel Society special on 19 March 1967.

A return visit on 20 February 2003 found one overgrown track still in position but no trace of the former passenger station. *Ian Holt/PDS*

PADIHAM POWER STATION began receiving coal by rail again in 1991 after a gap of more than a decade. The coal came from Maryport opencast disposal point in Cumbria and was conveyed in a daily trainload of PNA open box wagons, previously used for stone traffic. The inaugural train is pictured during unloading at Padiham on 16 November 1991, with No 60032 *William Booth* providing the traction. In the background is the oil discharge terminal, which had received occasional tank trains until the spring of 1991.

Unfortunately, the newly won coal traffic did not last long. Padiham power station closed in 1993 and the last trains on the branch were those carrying surplus coal away from the redundant stockpile. Shuttleworth Mead Business Park now occupies much of the power station site, but the eastern end was still awaiting development when visited on 20 February 2003. *Both PDS*

ROSE GROVE (1): The huge coaling tower of Rose Grove shed dominates the skyline as 'WD' 2-8-0 No 90320 heads east with a mixed rake of steel-bodied and wooden-bodied mineral wagons on 24 April 1951. The 24C shed plate shows that No 90320 was allocated to Lostock Hall. The 'WD' 2-8-0s were introduced in 1943 for the Ministry of Supply and purchased by British Railways in 1948.

Believe it or not, Rose Grove station is still operational. However, all passenger trains now call at the eastern end of the long island platform. The desolate view looking west is seen on 20 February 2003. *H. C. Casserley/PDS*

ROSE GROVE (2): An interesting assortment of railway-owned and privately-owned wagons line the sidings next to Rose Grove station as Hughes 5MT 2-6-0 No 42715 heads east with a mixed goods train on 24 April 1951.

The only railway presence at Rose Grove today is the unstaffed island platform for local trains to and from Colne. Those terraced houses nearest the photographer in the 'past' picture were demolished to make way for the M65 motorway, which also slices through the site of Rose Grove engine shed. The 'present' photograph is dated 29 March 2003. *H. C. Casserley/PDS*

BURNLEY CENTRAL (1): Although the Preston resignalling scheme of the early 1970s covered the whole of the Copy Pit line and even a short stretch of the Calder Valley line through Todmorden, it excluded the Colne branch beyond Gannow Junction; Burnley Central box, erected by the L&YR in 1900, therefore became the fringe box to Preston. A four-car DMU comprising cars M53443, M53493, M53525 and M53473 departs with the 1148 Colne-Preston service on 30 May 1983.

After the withdrawal of freight traffic, the remaining double track section to Chaffers Siding became a luxury for the hourly passenger service. The whole branch was reduced to a single-track 'siding' from Gannow Junction in December 1986. The 'present' scene is dated 20 February 2003. *Both PDS*

BURNLEY CENTRAL (2): The old market town of Burnley blossomed with the cotton industry, its population increasing from 25,000 in 1851 to over 100,000 in 1914. Its principal passenger station, Burnley Bank Top, was renamed Burnley Central in 1944 but was a rather modest facility for such a large town. Ex-LMS Hughes 2-6-0 No 42717 calls with the 12.55pm Colne-Manchester train on 24 April 1951.

New station buildings were provided in the 1960s but are now in poor condition. In 2002 the Strategic Rail Authority gave its backing to a £500,000 rebuilding scheme, including an enlarged car park and better facilities for buses and taxis. Single unit No 153310 arrives with the 1709 Colne-Blackpool South service on 26 May 2003. *H. C. Casserley/PDS*

BURNLEY CENTRAL (3): Burnley retained a rail-served coal concentration depot and National Carriers terminal until the late 1970s. Class 25 No 25082 performs shunting duties at the sidings just north of the passenger station on 16 September 1976. At that time the Class 25 fleet was almost intact, with more than 300 examples spread throughout the London Midland Region and parts of the Scottish and Western regions.

Today, a narrow strip of land suffices for the surviving single track north of Burnley. 'Pacer' No 142067 ambles along with the 1603 Blackpool South-Colne service on 26 May 2003. The Class 25s began to head for the scrapyard in quantity in 1980/81, and the last example was withdrawn from BR stock in 1987. *Michael Mensing/PDS*

COPY PIT: In the steam era the Copy Pit line from Todmorden (Hall Royd Junction) to Burnley (Gannow Junction) was a busy route for trans-Pennine freight, especially coal, and the gradients required the use of a banking locomotive on loaded trains. Stanier 8F 2-8-0 No 48053 pushes an unfitted coal train over the summit on 19 November 1966.

By the end of the 1970s the only trains routed via Copy Pit were Summer Saturday holiday trains. The line was proposed for closure in 1983, but gained an 11th-hour reprieve, and BR introduced an all-year-round passenger service over the line in October 1984. Freight returned in 1987 after a five-year gap, although it has since dwindled again. Unit No 158906 breasts the summit with the 1047 Blackpool North-York service on 20 February 2003. *Roger Siviter/PDS*

PORTSMOUTH: This superb piece of social history at Portsmouth station, on the Yorkshire side of Copy Pit summit, is believed to date from 1910. The line had been opened by the Manchester & Leeds Railway in 1849 to give that company a route to the East Lancashire towns and Preston.

The six intermediate stations between Hall Royd Junction and Gannow Junction were closed one by one from 1930 onwards. Portsmouth succumbed in 1958, while Burnley Manchester Road (since re-opened) was the last to go in 1961. The site of Portsmouth station is pictured on 20 February 2003. *John Ryan collection/PDS*

NELSON, CHAFFERS SIDING: The Colne branch was singled beyond Chaffers Siding after the Colne to Skipton link closed in 1970. The 1241 train from Colne to Preston approaches the double-track section at Chaffers Siding cabin on 30 May 1983, formed of Class 108 DMU cars M54246, M53982, M53963 and M54240.

Chaffers Siding cabin was downgraded to a gate box in 1986 and closed completely in 1991. The wooden level crossing gates were replaced by lifting barriers and the two footbridges over the line were removed. The crossing is now operated by the traincrew using a control wire and plunger. 'Pacer' No 142048 forms the 1309 Colne-Blackpool South service on 20 February 2003.

Chaffers Siding cabin was a Saxby & Farmer Type 8 structure dating back to 1876. The iron footbridge provided an alternative route for pedestrians when the gates were closed; it would have been well used when the local cotton mills were in full production.

The L&YR installed a new 24-lever frame in the cabin in 1904, and it remained in use until the cabin closed, but in later years some of the levers were taken out of use and painted white. *All PDS*

EARBY: The first line to reach Colne was the branch from Skipton via Earby, opened as an extension of the Leeds & Bradford Railway in 1848. It later became an unlikely outpost of the Midland Railway, meeting L&YR metals at Colne station to provide a through route across the Pennines. In this view facing Colne on 23 April 1954, the Barnoldswick branch train stands in the northbound platform. To start from this platform rather than from the branch platform on the opposite side of the station would have been a common procedure, as it avoided crossing both through lines to gain access to the Barnoldswick branch.

The Colne-Skipton line escaped the Beeching axe, but in 1968 it failed to attract the necessary subsidy and the last service on the line ran in January 1970. At Earby the trackbed is partly in use as a footpath, as pictured on 23 January 2003. A feasibility study carried out in 2003 effectively dashed hopes that the line might soon be re-opened, arguing that the social and economic benefits would not justify the projected re-opening cost of at least £30 million. *R. M. Casserley/PDS*

BARNOLDSWICK: The 1¾-mile branch from Earby opened in 1871 to serve the small manufacturing town of Barnoldswick. It was worked from the start by the Midland Railway, which perhaps explains why the junction at Earby faced Skipton rather than Colne. The LMS introduced motor train working on the branch in 1931 in an attempt to reduce costs, a practice that was to continue into BR days. LMS Class 3F 0-6-0 No 3477 stands at the single-platform terminus with the 8.55am to Earby on 11 June 1947.

The branch closed to passengers in 1965 and to goods in the following year. A visit on 23 January 2003 found the site occupied by a supermarket car-park. *H. C. Casserley/PDS*

The Fylde

The Fylde (a word derived from the Anglo-Saxon term 'gefilde' meaning 'plain') encompasses the area west of Kirkham & Wesham, from where there were three railway routes into Blackpool. The earliest was the Preston & Wyre Railway, which opened in July 1840 between Preston and Fleetwood, and was taken over jointly by the L&YR and LNWR in 1849. The port of Fleetwood was used by passengers travelling from London to Scotland via Ardrossan until the West Coast Main Line provided a direct rail link in 1848.

In 1846 the branch line from Poulton to Blackpool Talbot Road (to become Blackpool North in 1932) opened, which released the floodgates for visitors to the town. Although there had been a short branch to Lytham Dock it was not until 1863 that a separate line from Lytham to Blackpool opened, the two lines finally being connected at Lytham in 1874. The original terminus in Blackpool (Hound's Hill) was renamed Blackpool Central around 1878. In 1899 a curve was installed at Poulton, enabling trains to travel directly between Blackpool and Fleetwood.

A direct line from Kirkham & Wesham to Blackpool South opened in 1903, giving some relief to the increasingly busy approach via Lytham. By now Blackpool had grown hugely as a resort and had overtaken Southport as Lancashire's 'premier' holiday destination. North station had 15 platforms, and Central 14.

After the Second World War, the increase in coach and private car travel soon made inroads into the number of people arriving by rail. Central station closed in 1964, the direct line from Kirkham the year after and subsequently South station was reduced to a single-platform terminus. North became the principal station for Blackpool, having been rebuilt in 1974. The Fleetwood branch lost its passenger service in 1970 but remained open for freight to and from Burn Naze until 1999.

KIRKHAM & WESHAM (1): The station has always been the rail gateway to Blackpool and all traffic passes through, either stopping at the island platform or using the platform avoiding lines. Opened by the Preston & Wyre Railway as 'Kirkham' in 1840, it was renamed to its present title around 1906. On 21 July 1973 Class 25 locomotives Nos 7601 and 7607 head east with an express from Blackpool. On the right stands Kirkham Station signal box.

The island platform and buildings appeared much the same when visited on 1 August 2003, some 30 years after the 'past' photograph, although the station had an air of neglect. The booking office was boarded up, but at least First North Western had a revenue employee on duty in the morning, who could check and issue tickets. The signal box closed in 1975 and was subsequently demolished. Class 175 No 175112, operated by First North Western, enters the platform with the 0952 Blackpool North-Manchester Airport service. *Tom Heavyside/JCH*

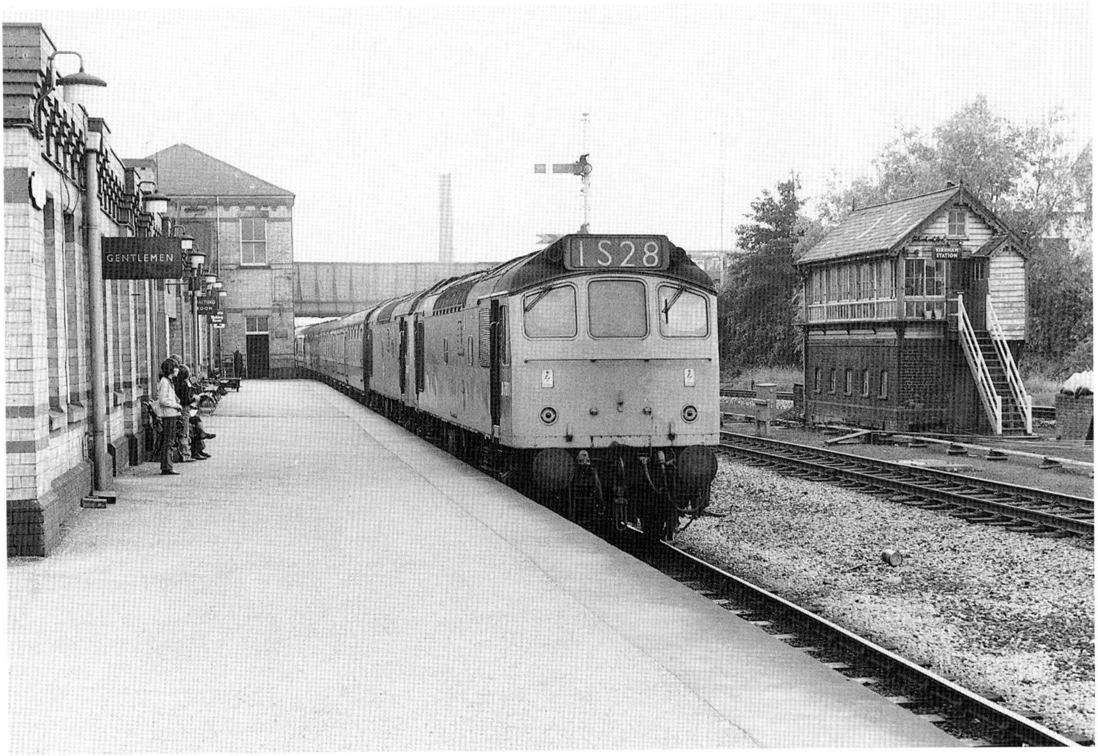

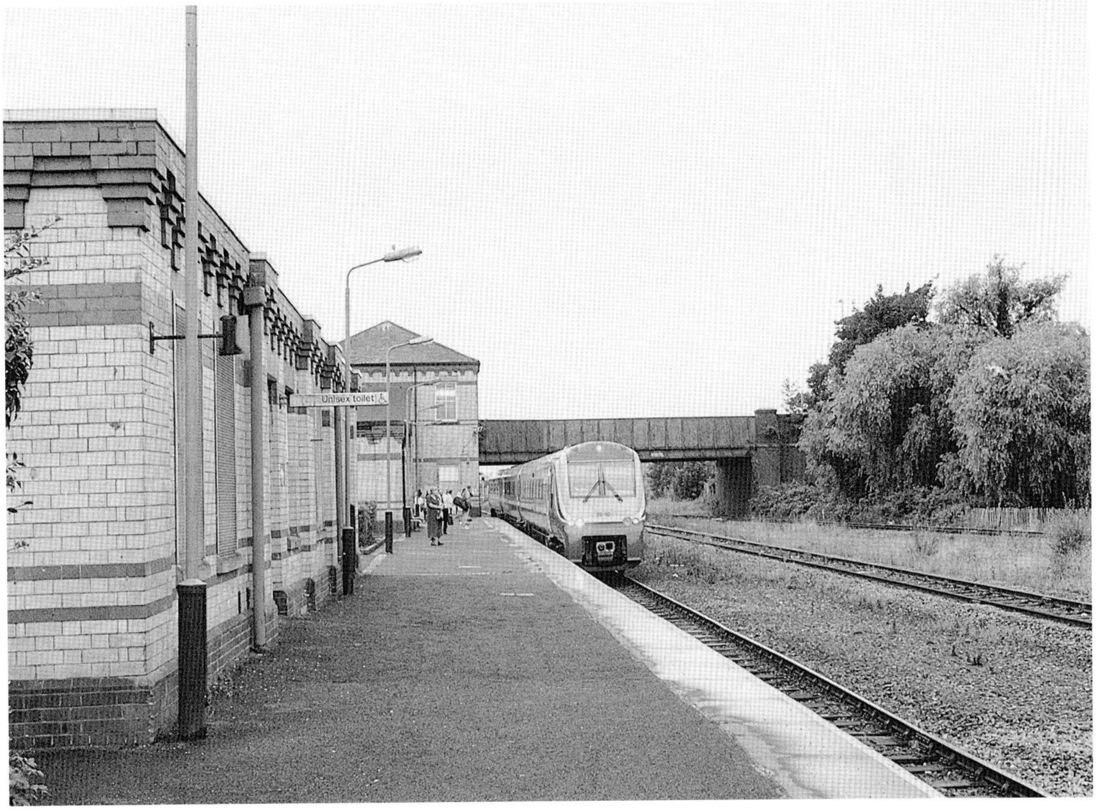

KIRKHAM & WESHAM (2): Looking east towards the station, this atmospheric photograph of around 1900 shows five smoking mill chimneys, including Parkinson's Biscuit Works (later Fox's) and Phoenix and Wesham Mills (both cotton). Although it is difficult to discern, there is a church steeple on the skyline above the distant train. The junction signal in the foreground on the down fast line applies to Poulton and Blackpool North (taller post) and to Blackpool South via St Annes-on-the-Sea (the Marton 'direct' line to Blackpool was not yet built).

On 4 September 2003 a number of changes are obvious, including track rationalisation and the loss of the semaphore signals. The only signal box is Kirkham North Junction, which is behind the photographer on the north side of the line. The area to the left has been completely redeveloped and now houses a modern Fox's biscuit factory, which gives off a mouth-watering aroma! The goods shed to the right remains, as does the church on the skyline. 'Sprinter' No 150223 heads towards the station with the 1352 Blackpool North-Manchester Airport service. *John Ryan collection/JCH*

ST ANNES-ON-THE-SEA: The first station was known as Cross Slack but was replaced by a second station, renamed St Annes-on-the-Sea, in 1875. The line was extremely busy and the station was substantially rebuilt in 1926. In our 'past' photo, a two-car DMU is on the down line heading for Blackpool South in the early 1980s, not long before the seaward-side platform buildings were demolished to make way for a supermarket.

On 1 August 2003 Class 142 No 142042 arrives with the 1009 service from Colne to Blackpool South. The change that has occurred within less than 20 years is remarkable, with just a small modern building having replaced the 1926 edifice. The Blackpool South branch is now single-track with no passing loops, so the current frequency of one train an hour cannot be increased. *The Gazette, Blackpool/JCH*

SQUIRES GATE station was a latecomer to the line, opened by the LMS in 1931 between St Annes-on-the-Sea and South Shore (Blackpool). As seen in the 'past' photograph, it had a handsome entrance, the building being shared with the District Bank at street level with steps leading down to the platforms.

The building has regrettably been demolished, probably when the line was singled in the 1980s. There is now no booking office, just the basic entrance to the remaining platform (the old down), as seen on 16 September 2003. The bridge stones bear a striking resemblance to the original station frontage buildings. *The Gazette, Blackpool/JCH*

BLACKPOOL SOUTH: Known as 'Waterloo Road' when opened in 1903, the station was renamed to its existing title by the LMS in 1932. In 1916 it became a junction when the new line from Kirkham via Marton was opened. On 21 May 1961 'Crab' 2-6-0 No 42732 is seen with the 6.38pm return excursion from Blackpool Central to Darwen, which will probably take the direct line to Kirkham.

All the stations on the branch from Kirkham via St Annes were reduced to single platforms in 1983. On 1 August 2003 Class 142 No 142068 forms a train to Colne, which is the destination for most services from this station. Over to the right is a reminder of the past, where the road overbridge indicates the former trackbed towards Blackpool Central. *D. Holmes/JCH*

BLACKPOOL CENTRAL SHED was opened in 1863 by the Blackpool & Lytham Railway as a four-road dead-end shed, together with turntable, water tank and coal stage. It was rebuilt by the L&YR in 1885 with eight dead-end roads and subsequently re-roofed by British Railways in 1957. Although closed in 1964, its demolition was delayed as it continued to service visiting engines for a while. In the photograph of 2 April 1961, we see two 4-6-0 'Black Fives', Nos 45411 and 44730, 4-6-0 'Jubilee' No 45559 *British Columbia* with 2-6-4T No 42546, together with an early sign of the future in Brush Type 2 (later Class 31) No D5689.

Today the whole area once occupied by the shed is part of a vast coach and car park, seen on 6 August 2003. The age of the Brush Type 2s has come and gone: No D5689 became No 31261 and was withdrawn in the mid-1980s. *D. Holmes/JCH*

BLACKPOOL CENTRAL (1): The bustling entrance to the station is seen during a summer season. There is a notice in the centre advising passengers that access to platforms 7-14 (the excursion platforms) is via Central Drive, to the left.
Following the closure of the station, the area around the entrance was completely redeveloped and no one would guess there was once an extremely busy station there. The 'present' scene was recorded on 16 September 2003. *The Gazette, Blackpool/JCH*

BLACKPOOL CENTRAL (2): This wonderful view taken from the top of the tower shows the full extent of the station with the excursion platforms to the left. Opened in 1863 simply as 'Blackpool', it changed to Hounds' Hill in 1878 and finally became Central in 1878. Right at the top can just be seen Central shed (to the left of the top of the chimney stack) and one of the signal boxes.

The 'present' photograph of 16 September 2003 was difficult to take because the view from the public area at the top of the Tower is obscured by protective netting – hence the horizontal rather than vertical format. The only part of the station that remains is the small block of buildings slightly left of centre, at the start of the huge car and coach park that continues to South station. Central Drive leads off to the left and the Promenade is on the extreme right, while careful examination of the two pictures reveals that a number of non-railway buildings have survived. *The Gazette, Blackpool/JCH*

BLACKPOOL CENTRAL (3): This photograph was taken immediately after closure of the station in November 1964. There is an eerie stillness – everything still intact but no trains, no people.

While the tower stands proud, virtually the whole station area has become an enormous car park. A number of buildings on the skyline are recognisable in the 'present' photograph dated 16 September 2003. *The Gazette, Blackpool/JCH*

POULTON-LE-FYLDE became a junction when the branch to Blackpool was opened from the Fleetwood line. Another connection was later put in between the two lines north of the station, forming a triangle and allowing through services between Blackpool and Fleetwood. Passenger services to Fleetwood were withdrawn in 1970, but the branch was kept open for freight to Fleetwood power station, Fleetwood coal concentration depot (until 1983) and Burn Naze. On 30 March 1989 Class 47 No 47319 waits at the signal on the Fleetwood line to proceed on to the main line with 6Z25, the 1325 Burn Naze-Lindsey oil empties.

In 1999 the last remaining freight flow from Burn Naze ceased and the branch was taken out of use, although, as seen in the 'present' picture of 6 August 2003, the track remains in situ. There were once five signal boxes at Poulton, but now only No 3 remains, dating back to 1896. Class 156 No 156455, allocated to Newton Heath depot (NH), approaches the box with the 0952 Blackpool North-Manchester Airport service. *PDS/JCH*

BLACKPOOL NORTH began life as simply 'Blackpool' when opened by the Preston & Wyre Railway in 1846, when what was then a branch line from Poulton opened. The first name change came in 1872 when it became known as 'Blackpool Talbot Road'. By 1898 the station had been rebuilt with an imposing entrance, which still stood when our 'past' picture was taken on 24 May 1972. Behind can be seen the curved tops of the fine train sheds. However, the wind of change was blowing and beyond the Victorian entrance can be seen several modern buildings.

By 1991 the station had been completely modernised, having survived the recommendation of closure by Dr Beeching, who wanted to keep Central station open instead. On 6 August 2003 nothing remains of the old station frontage, and the immediate area has been redeveloped. Behind the modern buildings is the entrance to the rebuilt station, seen in the third picture. *Ray Ruffell, Silver Link collection/JCH (2)*

THORNTON: There had been a station in the Thornton area since the early 1840s, the original being called 'Ramper' or 'Ramper Road'. In 1865 a new station named 'Cleveleys' was built on the south side of the crossing, becoming 'Thornton for Cleveleys' in 1905. This station was replaced by a third station to the north of the crossing in 1925, renamed 'Thornton-Cleveleys' in 1953. Passenger services were withdrawn in 1970. In the photograph dated 4 April 1985, Class 25 No 25181 heads 7P87, the 1043 Speedlink service from Walton Old Junction to Burn Naze.

After the end of freight in 1999, the line was taken out of use and, although the track from Poulton-le-Fylde remains in situ, it is very overgrown. As can be seen in the photograph of 16 September 2003, the signal box and semaphores have gone and there is no trace of the former station on the other side of the crossing. *PDS/JCH*

FLEETWOOD (1): The first station at Fleetwood was opened by the Preston & Wyre Railway in 1840, but it was replaced by a new one when the line was extended in 1883. An imposing Victorian building, opposite Queen's Terrace, it showed the railway company's confidence and optimism. Passengers were able to step straight from their train on to one of the ferries to Belfast or elsewhere. The date of our 'past' photograph is not known, but is likely to be about 1900.

Sadly, rail traffic diminished in the British Railways era and the station closed in 1966. Wyre Dock was upgraded as a substitute terminus for Fleetwood, but this too closed in 1970, ending all passenger traffic to the town. In today's photograph, taken on 6 August 2003, the area where the main station was situated is now partly taken up by retail outlets, although at the far end a pub called The Old Station recalls the railway. Beyond is a storage area for one of the shipping firms. *John Ryan collection/JCH*

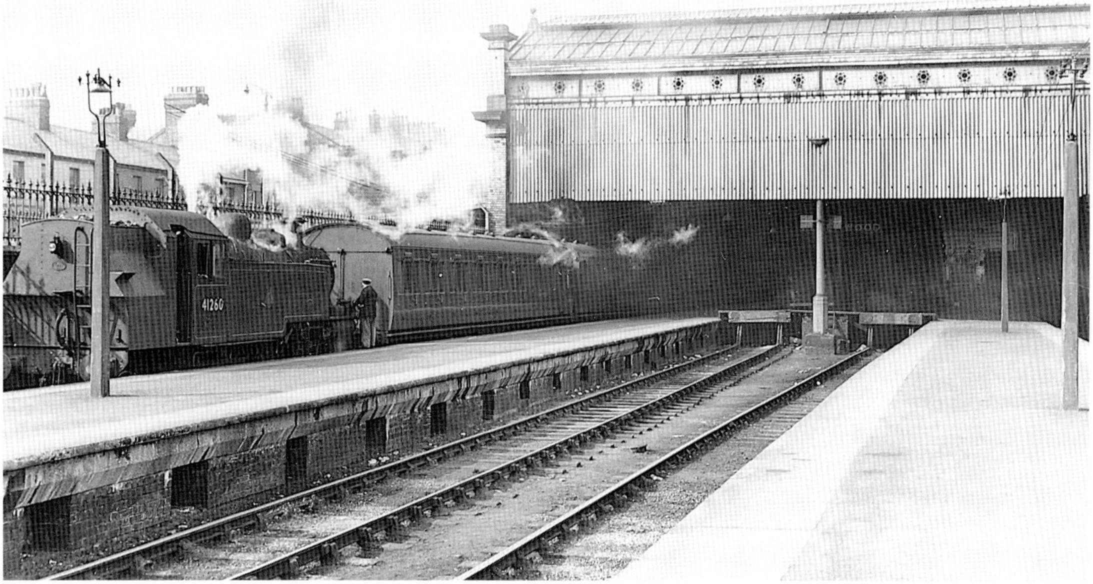

FLEETWOOD (2): In this view looking towards the buffers, taken in March 1955, Ivatt 2-6-2T No 41260 gently simmers in anticipation of departure time.

In the 'present' view, Queen's Terrace is to the left and further right can just be seen the attractive North Euston Hotel, which opened in 1841. At that time, before the opening of the West Coast Main Line, Fleetwood was on the shortest route from London to Glasgow via rail and sea (before the opening of the WCML). A best bedroom in 1843 cost the princely sum of 3s 15d – breakfast was extra! *R. M. Casserley collection/JCH*

Around Lancaster

The first railway in Lancaster was the Lancaster & Preston Railway, which opened in 1840, its services including through carriages to Euston Square. The end of 1846 saw the opening of the Lancaster & Carlisle Railway. In the same year the 'Little' North Western Railway was given royal assent for its branch connecting Skipton with Lancaster and Low Gill.

Two years later the line was opened from Lancaster Green Area (later 'Ayre') station to Poulton(-le-Sands), with enthusiastic backing from the Midland Railway, which was keen to establish a West Coast destination – Poulton later developed into the Victorian town of Morecambe. Late in 1849 a connection was opened between the Lancaster & Carlisle's Castle station and that at Green Area.

It was not long before the LNWR began to show an interest in the resort and built a branch from Hest Bank in 1864, initially using the Midland station, Poulton Lane, opened in 1870, then its own Euston Road in 1886. Later a connection was made north of Lancaster enabling trains to run to Morecambe direct without reversing at Hest Bank. The small harbour at Morecambe was found to be inadequate and this led to the Midland opening a line to Heysham, a new port offering much greater facilities, with connecting sailings primarily to Ireland.

The Midland opened its Promenade station at Morecambe in 1907 and in the following year electrified the line from Green Ayre, as well as the single-line connection to Castle station. This was one of the first examples of overhead rather than third-rail electrification.

Morecambe became a popular holiday destination and Heysham a well-used port, but decline started after the Second World War, with Green Ayre closing in 1966. Promenade station was closed and a much smaller one built a few hundred yards inland in 1994. The Heysham branch remains open for trains connecting with sailings to the Isle of Man and Belfast, while there is a healthy service of trains from Lancaster to Morecambe, including four trains a day from Leeds, perpetuating the Midland Railway connection.

GARSTANG & CATTERALL was one of six intermediate stations between Preston and Lancaster; it was also the junction for the Knott End branch. Although Garstang was a town of some importance, its main-line station was nearly 2 miles away and failed to attract large volumes of traffic. The station is pictured on 12 August 1967, looking towards Preston. The timetable of that period shows only a small number of trains booked to call, with long gaps during the middle of the day.

Garstang & Catterall closed to passengers in February 1969, goods traffic having ceased two months earlier. The 'present' photograph is dated 26 May 2003. *F. W. Shuttleworth, courtesy John Ward/PDS*

COGIE HILL: The Knott End branch was cut back to Pilling in 1950 – a final admission of defeat for the would-be port of Knott End. BR continued to operate a pick-up goods service to and from Pilling until 1963. 'Black Five' No 45019 passes the site of Cogie Hill halt with a typically lightly loaded working from Pilling on 21 June 1961. The 'M' prefix on the seven-plank wagon shows its LMS origin.

Much of the former Knott End branch has since returned to agriculture, but the remnants of a level crossing gate at Cogie Hill confirmed that this was the correct location when visited on 26 May 2003. *Noel A. Machell/PDS*

KNOTT END: The Garstang & Knot-End Railway was incorporated in 1864 but it was not until 1908 that the final stretch of the branch, from Pilling to Knott End, opened to traffic. When the railway was absorbed into the LMS in 1923 it owned four small tank engines, one of which – a Manning Wardle 0-6-0T named *Knott End* – is pictured at the terminus in pre-LMS days.

Knott End never grew as a seaport to rival Fleetwood, as the promoters of the GKER had hoped it would. Passenger services ceased in 1930 and the line between Pilling and Knott End closed completely in 1950. The station building at Knott End lived on as a café; it was rebuilt in 1994 with the addition of an upper storey. On 26 May 2003 there is no obvious trace of a railway having existed. *John Ward collection/PDS*

The third photograph shows a present-day reminder of the long-closed branch line: a Hudswell Clarke 0-6-0 saddle-tank in replica GKER livery residing at the entrance to Fold House Caravan Park near Pilling. This locomotive was built in 1955 and finished its working life at Mountain Ash in South Wales. *PDS*

LANCASTER CASTLE (1): The station has a history dating back to 1846, when it was opened by the Lancaster & Carlisle Railway. The name was simplified to just 'Lancaster' by British Railways in 1969, following the closure of Green Ayre in 1966. In our 'past' picture, dated 1 October 1965, a Morecambe to Lancaster Castle electric unit, headed by car No M28221M, approaches the station where it will terminate, before returning via Green Ayre to Morecambe.

On 29 August 2003 InterCity 125 power car No 43093 heads the 0855 Aberdeen to Penzance, with No 43094 bringing up the rear – this was just before Virgin Cross Country withdrew its last InterCity 125 workings. The line to Green Ayre branched off just to the right of the train. *Gavin Morrison/JCH*

LANCASTER CASTLE (2): On 8 August 1966 Ivatt 2-6-0 No 46486 is propelling a short train of vans to the yards south of the station, on the down platform road. The reason for this movement is that the vans (containing linoleum) have come from Lune Mills on the Glasson Dock branch, and the only connection from the branch on to the main line was via a facing junction from the down slow. Several of these engines were based at Lancaster shed, which was situated by Green Ayre station.

On 26 November 2003 Class 87 No 87016 *Willesden Intercity Depot* heads the 0830 London Euston-Glasgow service. Apart from the electrification, the scene has changed very little in the 36 years between the photographs. Had this been an up train, the locomotive would have been propelling, as it was normal practice for the engine to have been at the 'country' end of these trains. By the time this book is published it is likely that there will be few loco-hauled trains on the WCML as most services will have been taken over by 'Voyagers' and 'Pendolinos'.
Noel A. Machell/JCH

LANCASTER GREEN AYRE: Opened in 1848 as 'Lancaster', the station became 'Lancaster Green Area' and changed again to 'Lancaster Green Ayre' in 1870, by which time it was operated by the Midland Railway. In the view taken from the west end of the platform looking north, Austerity 2-8-0 No 90395 comes off the Greyhound Bridge across the River Lune with an up freight on 9 October 1965, only a few months before the station was closed for passenger traffic. Green Ayre closed to goods in 1968, but the connection from Castle station to Green Ayre remained open until 1976 for traffic to the power station at Ladies Walk.

Today nothing remains of the station and the bridge was transformed into a main road out of the city, known as Greyhound Bridge Road and leading to the A683 to Morecambe. The 'present' picture was taken on 29 August 2003. *Gavin Morrison/JCH*

LANCASTER GREEN AYRE SHED: Located just south of the station, the shed, opened in 1868 by the Midland Railway, consisted of four dead-end roads, diverging from a turntable. In this photograph of 9 October 1965, two Ivatt 2-6-0 engines, Nos 46431 and 46486, await their next turns of duty, both locos displaying the shed code 10J, which denoted Green Ayre depot.

The shed closed in 1966, with the building surviving as a youth centre until 1984, when it was demolished. On 29 August 2003 the view across the supermarket car park shows a prominent building in the distance, which also appears in the background of the 'past' photograph. *Gavin Morrison/JCH*

LANCASTER GREYHOUND BRIDGE: On 21 April 1963 Type 4 (later Class 40) No D323 crosses the River Lune at the rear of a diverted Glasgow-Birmingham train; in the foreground is the line that connected Green Ayre with Castle station. The train had left the West Coast Main Line at Hest Bank to Bare Lane, run to Morecambe (Promenade) for reversal and the attachment of a pilot engine (in this case an unidentified ex-LMS Class 5 4-6-0) before running to Lancaster Green Ayre, where a further reversal took place up the steeply graded Castle branch (with the former pilot engine banking) to regain the WCML at Castle station.

The section of track across Greyhound Bridge closed in 1967, but the bridge was retained and converted to a road. Although the cottages remain, foliage prevented the use of the same viewpoint on 4 September 2003. However, the bridge can be clearly seen behind the relatively new (and attractive) footbridges in the foreground. *Noel A. Machell/JCH*

BARE LANE station was opened as 'Poulton-le-Sands' in 1848 by the Morecambe Harbour & Railway (sic) and was renamed to its existing title in 1864. It was the only station on the branch. Our 'past' photograph of 3 March 1963 depicts Signalman Evans holding the single-line tablet for the secondman of Type 4 No D291 to collect before proceeding along the single line to Hest Bank, where the train will regain the WCML to continue its journey to Scotland. The service is an afternoon Manchester-Glasgow working, diverted due to engineering work on the Lune Viaduct. It had left the WCML at Lancaster Castle and descended to Green Ayre, where it had reversed, crossed the Greyhound Bridge and continued to Morecambe. The loco then ran round before rejoining the main line at Hest Bank Junction.

Today the line is operated in an unusual manner. From the single line east of the station, which becomes double from the station and beyond, the two single lines are operated as independent routes, making both platforms at Bare Lane bi-directional. In the picture of 19 August 2003, Class 142 No 142030 is approaching the old down platform with an up train, while No 142019 (on the right) heads for Morecambe, having just left the old up platform with a down train! *Noel A. Machell/JCH*

MORECAMBE PROMENADE (1): Opened by the Midland Railway in March 1907 with a true sea-front position, Promenade station replaced the old terminus at Northumberland Street. The Ordnance Survey map of 1913 shows a substantial station building with extensive tracks and carriage sidings close by, as well as a turntable and cattle dock sidings south of the station, with goods facilities by the side on the north side and the line running through to Morecambe Harbour. In this view of 28 May 1960, the posters advertise excursions to Barrow for 6 shillings, to Blackpool for 7s 6d and Southport for 8s 9d, together with one advising that the nearby former LNWR Euston Road station will be open from 13 June to 11 September.

Promenade station closed in 1994 and a much smaller modern station was opened a few hundred yards to the east. Fortunately the old station building was listed and remains much the same, now in use as an information and leisure centre. It was photographed on 19 August 2003. *T. J. Edgington/JCH*

HEYSHAM: At one time the Midland had a direct route from Lancaster Green Ayre to Heysham from its line to Morecambe, which could be accessed in either direction by means of a triangular junction. The original station opened in July 1904 as 'Heysham Harbour' and closed in 1970 when replaced by a new station on an adjacent site. The 'past' picture, taken on 31 May 1963, shows the extensive sidings around the docks as 'Black Five' 4-6-0 No 45212, working tender-first, pulls away past Heysham Harbour Junction signal box with the 10.30am Heysham Harbour-Crewe parcels train. The engine will run round its train at Morecambe Promenade and gain access to the WCML at Morecambe South Junction.

Our second photograph portrays an intermediate period. On 16 May 1987 a nine-coach unit headed by Class 108 No 51935 has just left the station forming the 1300m service to Stockport. The line to Heysham power station can just be seen on the left. The signal box in the previous picture has gone and been replaced by a more modern structure named Heysham Harbour.

Comparison with today (19 August 2003) shows that the line has been singled, the signal box having been removed for further use on the Dean Forest Railway, renamed Lydney Junction. The norm is for the passenger trains to be two-car units. In the summer timetable of 2003 there were two trains per day (Sundays included) to Heysham to connect with the 1415 ferry to Douglas, together with two more (Monday to Saturday only) to connect with a sailing to Belfast. The only freight is flask traffic from the nuclear power station. *Noel A. Machell/Tom Heavyside/JCH*

103

MORECAMBE PROMENADE (2): The first electric train service on the Morecambe branch dated back to 1908. In this view of 9 October 1965, a three-car unit headed by car No M29021M stands in the station with a service to Lancaster.

In the second picture, taken on 4 June 1988, the decline of the station has set in, although to the right the Art Deco-style Midland Hotel (opened in 1932) still looks to be cared for. A two-car Class 104 DMU, comprising Nos 53494 and 53468, is about to depart with the 1818 service to Lancaster.

By 19 August 2003 the area once occupied by tracks has been redeveloped into retail units and car-parks. One of the chimneys of the 1907 station building can still be seen. *Gavin Morrison/Tom Heavyside/JCH*

CARNFORTH (1): The present-day Carnforth station was opened by the LNWR and Furness Railway in 1880, replacing an earlier Lancaster & Carlisle Railway station dating back to 1846. The waiting room was the scene of the classic 1945 film *Brief Encounter* and has now been painstakingly restored to resemble its appearance in the film. On 22 June 1966, Class 5 4-6-0 No 45039 enters the down main-line platform with the 8.10am Preston-Windermere train. Semaphore signals, a water tank and water columns were all part of the everyday scene just two years before the end of steam.

The main-line part of Carnforth station closed in 1970 when BR withdrew stopping trains north of Lancaster on the West Coast Main Line. On 29 August 2003, looking south, we can see remnants of the platform as a Virgin 'Voyager' approaches with a down train. *H. C. Casserley/JCH*

CARNFORTH (2): Ex-LMS 2-6-2T No 40041 arrives with a train off the old Midland line from Yorkshire on 6 August 1960. Note the extensive point rodding and signal wires.

In the photograph of 4 September 2003 the goods shed and sidings have given way to an industrial estate, with subsequent simplification of trackwork. From Monday to Saturday there are five trains in each direction between Leeds/Skipton and Morecambe, with four on Sundays. *Keith Smith/JCH*

CARNFORTH MIDLAND SHED: Built on the north side of the line from Wennington, the Midland Railway opened its rectangular brick 'roundhouse' shed in 1874, and its facilities included a coal stage and water tank. In the photograph of 1932, ex-Midland 2-4-0 No 211 is in store in the foreground with a number of other elderly locos behind.

The shed was closed by the LMS in 1944 and its locomotives were transferred to the newly built depot beside Carnforth station. Today, however, the shed building remains virtually intact, used as offices and warehousing by private companies, as photographed on 29 August 2003. *John Ward collection/JCH*

WENNINGTON, on the line from Carnforth to Skipton, was once the junction for the direct line to Lancaster Green Ayre. In the 'past' photograph, taken on 12 September 1964, ex-LMS 'Jubilee' 4-6-0 No 45573 *Newfoundland* passes the signal box just west of the station with the 2.46pm Morecambe to Leeds service. The line to Carnforth goes off to the right under the roadbridge. The loco standing on the left is Fowler Class 4 2-6-4T No 42359 of Carnforth shed, waiting to back down on to the through Morecambe coaches off the 1.53pm Leeds to Carnforth, which split at Wennington.

The line to Green Ayre closed to passengers in 1966 and to freight in 1967. In today's picture, dated 4 September 2003, there is little sign of the former junction. Class 144 DMU No 144019 approaches the station with the 1022 Morecambe to Leeds service. The signal box looks in poor condition and on this occasion was 'switched out', so the signalling section extended from Carnforth Station Junction to Settle Junction. *Noel A. Machell/JCH*

HALTON station was opened in 1849 and lasted until 1966, when the passenger service between Lancaster Green Ayre and Wennington ceased. The station building was unique for the line in being built of brick; it was completed in 1907 after a passing train set fire to the original wooden structure. The photograph of 14 April 1963 shows ex-LMS 4-6-0 'Black Five' No 44758 slowing for the stop with a Leeds-Morecambe train.

On 4 September 2003 the station building on the former eastbound platform has survived well, and is in use as a storeroom. The railway ran on the south side of the River Lune and connection to the village on the opposite side was by means of a very narrow bridge, which at one time required payment of a toll. *Noel A. Machell/JCH*

Furness

The first stretches of the Furness Railway – from Barrow to Dalton and from Barrow to Kirkby-in-Furness – opened in 1846. Barrow at this time was just a small port with some 30 cottages. But the coming of the railway, and its subsequent extensions to Carnforth and Whitehaven, provided the means for Barrow to grow rapidly both as a port and as an industrial centre in its own right. By the early 1880s the town's population had risen to some 47,000, supported by a wide range of industries from shipbuilding and steel-making to paper manufacture and printing.

As the railway age progressed, the Furness Railway looked increasingly to tourism as well as industry for new traffic. The branch to Coniston, opened in 1859, targeted visitors to Coniston Lake as well as mineral traffic from Coniston Old Man, and the Lakeside branch, opened ten years later, provided direct interchange with pleasure steamers on Lake Windermere. Barrow itself, meanwhile, remained entirely industrial and acquired many miles of intricate goods lines and sidings, mostly in the docks area.

Early line closures included the Bardsea (Conishead Priory) branch in 1916 and the Piel (Roa Island) branch in 1936. The next casualties were the Coniston branch in 1962 and the Arnside-Hincaster Junction route in 1963. The Lakeside branch lost its all-year-round passenger service in 1939 but remained open for excursions until 1965. Its northernmost section from Haverthwaite to Lakeside was re-opened in 1973 as a privately run tourist railway.

Today even the 'main line' from Carnforth to Barrow and Whitehaven retains many relics from the pre-Grouping era, from the superb ironwork at Ulverston and Grange-over-Sands stations to the manual signal boxes at places such as Askam and Foxfield. By contrast, most traces of the former yards and sidings at Barrow Docks have disappeared; the only freight traffic handled at Barrow today is the occasional shipment of spent nuclear fuel for reprocessing at Sellafield.

ARNSIDE was still a junction when 'Black Five' 4-6-0 No 45394 was photographed heading for Carnforth with a solitary brake-van on 17 April 1968. But the 5¼-mile spur to Hincaster Junction on the West Coast Main Line had already been cut back to Sandside and was to close completely in 1971.
On 11 July 2003 'Coradia' unit No 175006 prepares to make its Arnside call with the 0800 Barrow-Manchester Airport service. The signal box remains in use, albeit partly obscured by a prefabricated hut, and the station building on the up platform seems in good repair. *Roger Siviter/PDS*

111

GRANGE-OVER-SANDS (1): The Ulverstone & Lancaster Railway (U&LR) brought the railway to Grange-over-Sands in 1857. The U&LR was absorbed in 1862 by the Furness Railway, which developed Grange as a 'Lancastrian riviera' and commissioned an attractive new station for the town. This undated postcard shows a Furness Railway 0-6-2 tank engine calling at the down platform.

The Furness Railway architecture at Grange was well cared for by a succession of railway operators and it now ranks as a Grade 2 listed building adjoining the town's conservation area. It was restored in 1997/98 by Railtrack, with financial contributions from the Railway Heritage Trust, North West Trains, English Heritage and three local councils. 'Coradia' unit No 175011 pauses for custom with the 0749 Manchester Airport-Barrow service on 11 July 2003. *John Ryan collection/PDS (3)*

GRANGE-OVER-SANDS (2): Stanier Class 5 4-6-0 No 45014 shunts the goods yard at Grange-over-Sands on 11 September 1958, the train being the Ulverston-Carnforth pick-up, which was usually worked by an ex-Midland 3F 0-6-0. The coal merchants' stock and weighing scales in the right foreground are worthy of note, as are the two camping coaches in front of the goods shed.

Grange goods yard closed in 1968, but through freight traffic continues to use the route today, including nuclear flask and chemical trains to and from Sellafield. Direct Rail Services locomotives Nos 37218 and 33025 top-and-tail a single empty caustic soda tank on 11 July 2003, forming 6F20, the 0825 from Sellafield to Runcorn Folly Lane. *Noel A. Machell/PDS*

GREENODD: The Furness Railway opened its 7½-mile Lakeside branch in 1869. It was designed mainly with tourism in mind, but also carried substantial quantities of freight, ranging from coal and iron-ore to gunpowder and bobbins. The branch was double-tracked as far as Greenodd, where it crossed the Leven estuary and continued as a single line to Haverthwaite and Lakeside. This Edwardian view of Greenodd shows the curved bridge, built for double track but only ever carrying a single track, with a long private siding running behind the row of houses.

After the branch closed, part of the trackbed was turned into the re-aligned A590 road, obscured by trees in this photograph dated 11 July 2003. Two of the buildings in the 'past' view are visible in the foreground. *John Ryan collection/PDS*

LAKESIDE (1): Regular, all-year-round passenger services on the Lakeside branch finished in 1938, but summertime excursion traffic continued until 1965. Metropolitan-Vickers Co-Bo No D5708 stands at the already rationalised terminus on 21 September 1963.

With its terminus on the shore of Lake Windermere providing direct connections with pleasure steamers, the Lakeside branch was an obvious candidate for preservation. The track on the whole branch was left in position until 1971, and the 3-mile stretch from Haverthwaite to Lakeside was restored to use in 1973. With the signal post from the first photograph still in position, Bagnall 0-6-0ST industrial locomotive *Princess* prepares to depart for Haverthwaite on 11 July 2003. *Princess* was built in 1942 and was formerly employed at Preston Docks. *Gavin Morrison/PDS*

LAKESIDE (2): All three platform faces at Lakeside were still in use when the 'past' scene was recorded on 29 May 1960. The stock from an incoming Stephenson Locomotive Society excursion stands well down the platform while its locomotive – Stanier taper-boiler 6P5F 2-6-0 No 42952 – runs round on the adjacent track.

On 11 July 2003 the passengers arriving on the first service of the day from Haverthwaite, hauled by 0-6-0ST *Princess*, disperse to catch a Windermere steamer or buy souvenirs at the local shop. The station has lost its overall roof but retains some of its original buildings. *T. J. Edgington/PDS*

ULVERSTON was something of a showpiece station for the Furness Railway, boasting elaborate iron and glass canopies with 'FR' monogrammed brackets and an imposing station building and clock tower. This view, facing Carnforth and dated approximately 1908, shows the unusual platform arrangement at Ulverston, designed to make it easier for passengers to change into and out of Lakeside branch connections.

Like Grange-over-Sands, Ulverston station is Grade 2 listed and was restored by Railtrack. Unit No 156424 departs as the 1432 Liverpool Lime Street-Barrow service on 11 July 2003. The foot crossing with steps part way along the platform is a curious, if not unique, feature.

The third picture shows the tastefully restored canopy and building on the down platform. It is just possible to make out the distinctive 'squirrel' motif on the platform benches. *R. M. Casserley collection/PDS (2)*

PLUMPTON JUNCTION originally marked the divergence of two branch lines: to Lakeside in the north and to Conishead Priory in the south. The service to Conishead Priory ceased as early as 1916, but a short stretch of the former branch remained in use to serve a Glaxo chemicals plant until 1994. Class 47 No 47119 passes the Glaxo branch junction with the 9T63 local trip working from Barrow-in-Furness to Carnforth on 1 August 1985. The train is running 'Class 9' with a brake-van because it comprises a mixture of air-braked and vacuum-braked wagons.

Plumpton Junction signal box was abolished in 2000 and the remaining semaphore signals were removed. Direct Rail Services locomotives Nos 37608 and 20315 pass the former junction on their way back to Sellafield on 11 July 2003. *Both PDS*

BARROW-IN-FURNESS: Located on the 1882-built loop line from Salthouse Junction to Thwaite Flat (later Park South Junction), Barrow-in-Furness was the largest station on the Furness Railway, designed in 'Swiss chalet' style with a striking timber framework and high roof. Ex-LNWR 'Waterloo' Class 2-4-0 No 5104 *Woodlark* and ex-Furness Railway 4P 4-6-4T No 11102 head an eastbound local passenger train in 1931. Both locomotives were nearing the end of their working lives: *Woodlark* was withdrawn in the autumn of 1931 and No 11102 lasted until 1934.

Barrow-in-Furness was a prime target during the Second World War and the station was destroyed during an air raid in the spring of 1941. It was left to British Railways to complete a replacement structure in 1957. Unit No 156460 waits to form the 1326 departure to Preston on 11 July 2003, while a second Class 156 unit has just arrived in the same platform on a Cumbrian Coast service. *John Ward collection/PDS*

BARROW DOCKS: An intricate network of lines and sidings once served the docks at Barrow-in-Furness. By the 1980s most of the rail activity had ceased, but a branch alongside Buccleuch Dock still served two coal depots – Cart and Hackett. Class 25 No 25221 positions a rake of HTV coal hoppers (and one MCV mineral wagon) in Hackett siding on 14 July 1983. It will then proceed down the branch to shunt Cart depot, just visible on the far left.

Neither Cart nor Hackett was equipped to handle modern air-braked wagons and both depots closed to rail traffic in 1984. The vacant trackbed is pictured on 11 July 2003. The only rail freight movements at Barrow at the time of writing are imported nuclear flasks at Ramsden Dock. *Both PDS*

BARROW SHIPYARD: From 1899 until 1966 Vickers shipyard workers had their own station at Island Road, reached by a spur from the Ramsden Dock branch. Services reached a climax during the Second World War with five daily return workings, each carrying between 10 and 12 coaches. Fowler 4F 0-6-0 No 44347, displaying shedplate 12E (Barrow), stands at Island Road with the Furness Rail Tour on 27 August 1961. This tour was organised jointly by the Stephenson Locomotive Society and the Manchester Locomotive Society.

The station and spur closed in December 1966, when Buccleuch Dock bridge was declared unsafe. BR diverted the remaining unadvertised workmen's trains to Barrow Central. On 11 July 2003 a shallow cutting provides a reminder of the former railway. *Noel A. Machell/PDS*

ASKAM station is pictured in Furness Railway days, with a northbound train departing towards Foxfield. The signal box guarding the level crossing is a typical Furness Railway structure, erected in 1890 and containing a 22-lever frame.

Roughly a century has passed and the station is remarkably unchanged. The most obvious alterations are the new level crossing barriers, the location boxes on both sides of the line, the tall lighting masts on the platforms and the spiked metal fencing on the left. The FR signal box still controls semaphores, although they are now of upper-quadrant type. The 'present' scene is dated 12 July 2003. *John Ryan collection/PDS*

FOXFIELD began life as an intermediate station on the Furness Railway extension from Kirby-in-Furness to Broughton, opened in 1848. It became a junction ten years later, when the Whitehaven & Furness Junction Railway installed a south-facing curve from its Whitehaven-Broughton line. The station was rebuilt in 1879 with a partially covered island platform and contiguous goods shed. It was still intact on 4 September 1954 when Fowler 4MT 2-6-4T No 42364 was photographed on the 5.30pm local from Barrow to Millom.

The Cumbrian Coast line is a low priority for resignalling and Foxfield retains its Furness Railway signal box, built in 1879 and extended in 1909 to house a 51-lever frame. Its largely wooden construction was intended to blend with the adjacent buildings. Another surviving relic is the water tank on the left, built from Coniston stone. Unit No 156426 calls with the 1710 Barrow-Carlisle service on 11 July 2003. *T. J. Edgington/PDS*

BROUGHTON: Originally the meeting place of lines from Barrow and Whitehaven, Broughton became an intermediate station on the Coniston branch after the north-facing curve at Foxfield was abandoned. The station staff stand proudly for the photographer in this delightful turn-of-the-20th-century scene.

After the Coniston branch closed in 1962, the trackbed at Broughton was sold off and developed as a housing estate. However, the station building still stands and now forms a private house. Its gable ends can just be seen in this view of 11 July 2003. *John Ryan collection/PDS*

CONISTON: The Coniston branch was opened in 1859 with two contrasting sources of business in mind: tourists visiting the Lake District and copper-ore from the slopes of Coniston Old Man; a single-track spur extended beyond the station to serve the ore mines. The 'Swiss chalet' station was designed by Edward Paley; it was enlarged in 1888 and again in 1896 to cater for growing traffic. Little appears to have changed since the late Victorian era in this view facing north on 8 August 1958.

The branch passenger service just failed to reach its centenary, coming to an end in October 1958, although a three-times-weekly goods service persisted until April 1962. Coniston station was demolished soon afterwards and the site is now occupied by houses and garages, as pictured on 11 July 2003. *R. M. Casserley/PDS*

INDEX OF LOCATIONS

Accrington 59-60; shed 58
Ainsdale 11
Ainsdale Beach 4-5
Arnside 111
Askam 124

Bacup 54; shed 53
Bare Lane 100
Barnoldswick 73
Barrow-in-Furness 121
 Docks 122
 Shipyard 123
Baxenden 57
Birkdale Palace 14
Blackburn 44-47
Blackpool Central 81-84; shed 80
Blackpool North 86
Blackpool South 79
Blundellsands & Crosby 9
Broughton 126
Burnley Central 65-67
Burscough Bridge 16
Burscough Junction 21

Carnforth 105-106; Midland shed 107
Clitheroe 50
Cogie Hill (GKER) 92
Coniston 127
Cop Lane, Penwortham 25
Copy Pit 68

Deepdale 35

Earby 72

Farington 27-28
Fleetwood 88-89
Formby 10
Foxfield 125

Garstang & Catterall 91
Grange-over-Sands 112-114
Great Harwood 51
Greenodd 115
Grimsargh 36

Halton 109
Haslingden 56
Heysham 102-103
Hoddlesden Junction 40
Hoghton 42

Kirkham & Wesham 75-76
Knott End 93

Lakeside 116-117
Lancaster Castle 6, 94-95
Lancaster Green Ayre 96-99; shed 97
Langho 49
Leyland 26
Longridge 38
Lostock Hall 29-30
Lower Darwen 41

Mill Hill 43
Morecambe Promenade 101, 104

Nelson, Chaffers Siding 70-71

Ormskirk 22

Padiham 61-62
Penwortham Cop Lane 25
Plumpton Junction 120
Portsmouth 69
Poulton-le-Fylde 85
Preston 32-34; East Lancs station 31

Rose Grove 63-64
Rufford 20

St-Annes-on-the-Sea 77
Southport Central 19
Southport Chapel Street 12-13, 17
Southport L&YR shed 18
Southport Lord Street 15
Squires Gate 78

Thornton 87
Town Green 23

Ulverston 118-119

Wardleworth 52
Waterfoot 55
Wennington 108
Whittingham Mental Hospital 37
Wilpshire 48